Using Mentor Texts to Teach Writing With the Traits
Middle School

RUTH CULHAM • JAMES BLASINGAME • RAYMOND COUTU

New York • Toronto • London • Auckland • Sydney
Mexico City • New Delhi • Hong Kong • Buenos Aires

Teaching *Resources*

To Margaret Blasingame (1928–1986), Don Emblen (1918–2009), and Catherine Branagan (1901–1980) who believed all children are special and all children can learn.

Credits:

Page 7: Promotional letter for *Catching Fire*, printed with permission of David Levithan.

Page 67: From *The Absolutely True Diary of a Part-Time Indian* by Sherman Alexie. Copyright © 2007 by Sherman Alexie. By permission of Little, Brown and Company.

Page 85: From *The Blue Star* by Tony Earley. Copyright © 2008 by Tony Earley. By permission of Little, Brown and Company.

Page 114: © 2003 Mark Parisi, www.offthemark.com, printed with permission.

Every effort has been made to find the authors and publishers of previously published material in this book and to obtain permission to print it.

Editor: Raymond Coutu
Cover and Interior Designer: Maria Lilja
Copy Editor: Eileen Judge

ISBN-10: 0-545-13843-4
ISBN-13: 978-0-545-13843-7

2 3 4 5 6 7 8 9 10   40   14 13 12 11

Contents

Introduction 4

Chapter 1: Ideas 12

Mentor Texts for
  Finding a Topic 14
  Focusing the Topic 17
  Developing the Topic 19
  Using Details 22

Focus Lessons for
  Finding a Topic 25
  Focusing the Topic 26
  Developing the Topic 28
  Using Details 30

Chapter 2: Organization 32

Mentor Texts for
  Creating the Lead 34
  Using Sequence Words and
  Transition Words 36
  Structuring the Body 39
  Ending With a Sense of Resolution 41

Focus Lessons for
  Creating the Lead 44
  Using Sequence Words
  and Transition Words 46
  Structuring the Body 47
  Ending With a Sense of Resolution 49

Chapter 3: Voice 52

Mentor Texts for
  Establishing a Tone 54
  Conveying the Purpose 57
  Creating a Connection
  to the Audience 59
  Taking Risks to Create Voice 62

Focus Lessons for
  Establishing a Tone 64
  Conveying the Purpose 66
  Creating a Connection
  to the Audience 68
  Taking Risks to Create Voice 70

Chapter 4: Word Choice 72

Mentor Texts for
  Applying Strong Verbs 74
  Selecting Striking Words and Phrases 77
  Using Specific and Accurate Words 79
  Choosing Words That Deepen Meaning ... 82

Focus Lessons for
  Applying Strong Verbs 85
  Selecting Striking Words and Phrases 87
  Using Specific and Accurate Words 88
  Choosing Words That Deepen Meaning ... 90

Chapter 5: Sentence Fluency 92

Mentor Texts for
  Crafting Well-Built Sentences 94
  Varying Sentence Types 97
  Capturing Smooth and
  Rhythmic Flow 99
  Breaking the "Rules"
  to Create Fluency 102

Focus Lessons for
  Crafting Well-Built Sentences 105
  Varying Sentence Types 107
  Capturing Smooth and
  Rhythmic Flow 109
  Breaking the "Rules"
  to Create Fluency 112

Chapter 6: Conventions 114

Mentor Texts for
  Checking Spelling 116
  Punctuating Effectively and
  Paragraphing Accurately 119
  Capitalizing Correctly 122
  Applying Grammar and Usage 124

Author Index 127

Title Index 127

References 128

Introduction

Every time we read their work, good writers teach us something about how the craft of writing works. When a writer digs deeply into a topic and provides fresh information about it, we think, "Wow! I didn't know that." That's the ideas trait in action. When a writer catches us up in the moment and connects to us, we think, "I love being in this space and I'm not budging until I've had my fill." That's the voice trait. When a writer invites us into the piece with an engaging introduction followed by a logically structured body, we think, "I'm hooked. This is adding up to something big." That's the organization trait. When a writer uses exquisite language that flows across the page, we think, "The perfect words in just the right places made that passage sing." That is the word choice and sentence fluency traits at work. And when a writer uses conventions so clearly and artfully that we don't even notice them, we think, "I got through that easily. There were no places where I got bogged down because of careless editing." That's conventions.

As readers, we make judgments like these every time we read a well-written piece. As writers, we can learn from reading, especially by trying what other writers accomplish successfully. Or as researcher Pilar Duran Escribano (1999) says, "Reading puts the learner in touch with other minds so that he can experience the ways in which writers have organized information, selected words and structured arguments" (p. 62). So who better to teach us how to write than those who have honed their craft and published extraordinary books for us to use as mentor texts in our work with young people? Lynne Dorfan and Rose Cappelli (2007), authors of *Mentor Texts: Teaching Writing Through Children's Literature, K–6*, define mentor texts as "pieces of literature that we can return to again and again as we help our young writers learn how to do what they may not yet be able to do on their own" (p. 2). We've long believed in the power of well-written texts. Students' rapt attention when a great piece of literature is shared is evidence of the book's quality. Couple that interest with students' attempts to imitate the author's moves and you have a powerful teaching strategy.

In this book, we bring you 150 fiction and nonfiction mentor texts by master writers, organized by trait—ideas, organization, voice, word choice, sentence fluency, and conventions. In each annotation, we explain what the text is about and why it's a good model for teaching a key quality of the target trait. We also provide lessons based on 20 of the mentor texts, with passages from those texts, that you can implement immediately. For more on what this book contains, see page 11.

Defining the Traits for Middle School Writers

Of course, before students can begin to see the traits at play in mentor texts, they need to know what they are. The traits are qualities of writing that, ideally, we all should consider when crafting a piece—any type of piece, whether it's a story, blog entry, or letter to the president.

Most middle schoolers do not have control over these critical writing skills, but they are well on their way, especially if they've been fortunate enough to have learned about the traits in elementary school. To make the traits as clear and comprehensible to students as possible, and to give you concrete topics for instruction, we've broken each one down into four essential characteristics, or "key qualities." (See next page.)

The key qualities allow us to get inside a trait and learn what makes it tick. Teaching the concept of "ideas," for instance, may be overwhelming to you. But teaching students how to find a topic, focus the topic, develop the topic, and use details probably isn't—and by teaching those skills using mentor texts, you not only help students understand the trait of ideas, you show them specifically what real writers do. Knowing the traits and their key qualities, and finding mentor texts that illustrate what they look like in the hands of experts, helps you show students what they need to do to make their writing strong.

The Traits of Writing

Ideas: The piece's content—its central message and details that support that message.

Organization: The internal structure of the piece—the thread of logic, the pattern of meaning.

Voice: The tone and tenor of the piece—the personal stamp of the writer, which is achieved through a strong understanding of purpose and audience.

Word Choice: The specific vocabulary the writer uses to convey meaning and enlighten the reader.

Sentence Fluency: The way words and phrases flow through the piece. It is the auditory trait because it's "read" with the ear as much as the eye.

Conventions: The mechanical correctness of the piece. Correct use of conventions (spelling, capitalization, punctuation, paragraphing, and grammar and usage) guides the reader through the text easily.

Noticing what a professional writer does, naming it, and showing students how to do it in their own work are essential to their success. Good writing happens over time, with lots of practice, lots of support, and lots of models. The traits give you the language to move students forward, step by step. Mentor texts give you the fuel to keep them going. It's a perfect match.

Key Qualities of Each Trait

Ideas
* Finding a Topic
* Focusing the Topic
* Developing the Topic
* Using Details

Word Choice
* Applying Strong Verbs
* Selecting Striking Words and Phrases
* Using Specific and Accurate Words
* Choosing Words That Deepen Meaning

Organization
* Creating the Lead
* Using Sequence Words and Transition Words
* Structuring the Body
* Ending With a Sense of Resolution

Sentence Fluency
* Crafting Well-Built Sentences
* Varying Sentence Types
* Capturing Smooth and Rhythmic Flow
* Breaking the "Rules" to Create Fluency

Voice
* Establishing a Tone
* Conveying the Purpose
* Creating a Connection to the Audience
* Taking Risks to Create Voice

Conventions
* Checking Spelling
* Punctuating Effectively and Paragraphing Accurately
* Capitalizing Correctly
* Applying Grammar and Usage

Finding Mentor Texts

Mentor texts are everywhere. We find them all the time as we read books, newspapers, magazines, and other types of print and electronic texts. Here's an example. Recently, an ARC (advance reader's copy) of a book we've been anxiously awaiting arrived at our doorsteps—*Catching Fire*, the second book in Suzanne Collins's Hunger Games trilogy. (We've included the first book, *The Hunger Games*, in the chapter on word choice because of Collins's fine use of language to create a new and very disturbing world.)

Included with *Catching Fire* was a letter from the editor, David Levithan. Our first reaction was sheer joy at having the new book followed by excitement at knowing the letter was ideal to share with students to illustrate the voice trait.

Dear Very Deserving, Very Lucky Reader,

You are about to make just about everyone I know very jealous. Not just every teenager that I know. No, more than that. I have been offered many things for this ARC. Some of them illegal. Many of them creative. But with fortitude I didn't know I particularly had, I kept the curtain drawn. Until now.

I don't really need to tell you why everyone's going to be so jealous, do I? Instead, I must beg you to keep quiet. Believe me, this isn't going to be easy. I've been living with these secrets for months now, and I can guarantee the minute you put this book down (and, I assure you, you won't put it down until it's over), you are going to want to talk to everyone you know about it. Just *please* don't ruin the surprises. Share your reaction? Certainly. But I implore you not to share the twists and turns. Allow everyone else the same privilege that is being afforded you—namely, the exquisite pleasure of opening a much-anticipated book without knowing what's going to happen once you're inside.

If you've made it to this third paragraph before opening this beautiful ARC, I admire your restraint. You can stop listening to me now. Katniss is waiting for you.

David Levithan
VP/Editorial Director

This letter clearly shows that connections between reading and writing can be powerful and can underscore the importance of writing well. Keep your eyes open for models of good writing—you'll discover them in all parts of life—and mark particularly good passages in them for use later. Because of time and space restrictions, we've limited this bibliography's selections to picture books, chapter books, and young adult novels. Consider these selections a starter set of models. In time, we're confident you'll add to it with all types of texts. We couldn't agree more with Katie Wood Ray (1999), author of *Wondrous Words*, who says, "Writing well involves learning to attend to the craft of writing, learning to do the sophisticated work of separating what it's about from how it is written" (p. 10).

Thinking About How Professional Writers Work: Passages to Ponder

Just as there is no single way to teach writing, there is no single way to write. However, most writers use a process approach of some sort that requires drafting, sharing, revising, and editing—and lots of thinking and rethinking. Share with students the following passages from bestselling authors Stephen King, Anne Lamott, and Bruce Brooks to get them contemplating how writers work, have them answer the questions that follow, and discuss their responses.

Stephen King from *On Writing: A Memoir of the Craft*

"Once I start work on a project, I don't stop and I don't slow down unless I absolutely have to. If I don't write every day, the characters begin to stale off in my mind—they begin to *seem* like characters instead of real people. The tale's narrative cutting edge starts to rust, and I begin to lose my hold on the story's plot and pace. Worst of all, the excitement of spinning something new begins to fade. The work begins to feel like work, and for most writers that is the smooch of death. Writing is at its best—always, always, always—when it is a kind of inspired play for the writer. I can write in cold blood if I have it, but I like it best when it's fresh and almost too hot to handle" (2000, p. 148).

- Can you describe your writing process? Do you tend to write quickly, slowly, or someplace in between?
- What is your favorite kind of writing?
- What does King mean by the phrase "inspired play"?

Anne Lamott from *Bird by Bird: Some Instructions on Writing and Life*

"Writing has so much to give, so much to teach, so many surprises. That thing you had to force yourself to do—the actual act of writing—turns out to be the best part. It's like discovering that while you thought you needed the tea ceremony for the caffeine, what you really needed was the tea ceremony. . . .

Ever since I was a little kid, I've thought that there was something noble and mysterious about writing, about the people who could do it well, who could create a world as if they were little gods or sorcerers. All my life I've felt that there was something magical about people who could get into other people's minds and skin, who could take people like me out of ourselves and then take us back to ourselves. And you know what? I still do" (1994, pp. xxvi-xxvii).

- Have you ever learned something as you were writing? What was it?
- Did that surprise you? Why?
- What part of writing is difficult for you?
- Is there a writer who gets "inside your mind and skin"? How does he or she do that?

Bruce Brooks from *Speaking for Ourselves: Autobiographical Sketches by Notable Authors of Books for Young Adults*

"No teacher ever saw my writing, but if one had read something such as *The Golf Course at Night* (a title I recall), he or she would have looked ahead to my future and said, "This boy, someday, is going to make an absolutely first-rate *accountant*." Or third-rate auto mechanic or something—anything but a writer, because the stories were so awful no one would have given me a hope. But the important thing, I suppose, was that I had the initiative to write them. I was not impatient. I knew they were bound to be bad for a while. I just kept practicing. And after only twenty more years of practice (who's counting?), I was ready to write a novel, which turned out to be *The Moves Make the Man*." (1990, p. 34).

- If you look into your future, what do you see? What do you see yourself writing?

- What role does initiative play in becoming a good writer—or a good anything, for that matter?

- Why do you think Brooks kept writing, even when he knew he wasn't good at it?

Understanding How the Traits Work Together: An Introductory Lesson

In our teaching, we should examine each trait in close detail, key quality by key quality. At the same time, it's important to remember we're teaching writing, not "traiting." So it's critical to keep the big picture clearly in mind also as we teach students how to use the traits to make their writing strong. Carry out this introductory lesson to clarify the role of the traits in the writing process.

Seven Blind Mice
Ed Young

Lesson Focus:

In this fable, the seven blind mice explore sections of what turns out to be an elephant. However, none of the mice figures that out until they put all their ideas together and realize that each of their smaller parts adds up to something bigger. Writers do the same thing as they look for the perfect idea for writing. They find pieces of information or develop parts of a story line, but until they put it all together, it doesn't add up to a whole idea. In this lesson, students explore the main idea of the story and compare it to the writing traits.

Materials:

- a copy of *Seven Blind Mice*
- projections of selected illustrations and pages
- list of the traits and their definitions, page 5
- paper, pens, pencils

What to Do:

1. Tell students you are going to read a story that is a fable, a story that features animals, plants, inanimate objects or forces of nature that are humanized. The fable has a strong moral lesson. Explain that this fable can be interpreted in two ways, literally (accept it at face value) or figuratively (dig into it for deeper meaning).

2. Tell students that writers often use similes and metaphors to make comparisons with strong imagery. A simile uses the words *like* or *as* in the comparison, a metaphor does not. For example, "He was as hungry as a bear," is a simile. However, "He was a bear at every mealtime," is a metaphor.

3. Read the story aloud using a document camera if possible, so everyone can see the text and the award-winning illustrations. Otherwise, show illustrations as you read. Pause after each blind mouse declares what he thinks "the strange Something that was discovered by the pond" is. Ask students to turn to a partner and talk about what the mouse thinks he "sees" and what it actually is. For instance, when the first mouse thinks he sees a pillar, it's actually an elephant leg and foot.

4. Project the list of the traits and their definitions, and review them quickly. Ask students to think about how the idea in the story compares to the traits of writing. Students should note that the mice did not know the Something was an elephant until they had all of the parts. In writing, all the traits are needed to make the work solid and effective. Writers need organization, voice, word choice, sentence fluency, and conventions, not just an idea, to craft well-developed, complete pieces.

5. Put students into pairs and ask them to create a simile that compares the moral of *Seven Blind Mice* ("Knowing in part makes a fine tale, but wisdom comes from seeing the whole.") to using the traits of writing. Here is an example: Wisdom comes from seeing the whole just as using every trait makes writing great.

6. Explain to students that, throughout the year, you will be showing them examples of strong writing, such as *Seven Blind Mice*, that show the traits in action, so students can learn the craft of writing from experts.

Lesson Extension:

Put students into groups of two or three and ask them to create lists of other things in which the sum of their parts is bigger than the parts themselves, such as a winning sports team, a delicious meal, or a world-class symphony. Ask group members to share with the class how the whole is more important than its individual elements.

An Invitation to Explore: What This Book Contains and How to Use It

The cornucopia of books we've assembled here is only a taste of the many mentor texts available to you. But, to us, they are among the best, representing a wide range of flavors and textures. We devote a chapter to each writing trait. Within each chapter, we present six mentor texts for every key quality—two picture books, two chapter books, and two young adult novels. Each text is annotated to give you a sense of what it is about and how it could be used to teach writing.

You'll find that some of the young adult novels we've selected have mature themes related to sexuality, violence, and substance abuse, as indicated at the end of their annotations. We recommend these books because of the high quality of the writing and to give middle school students an opportunity to read about topics that may be impacting their own lives somehow. We're not promoting these themes by any means—after all, reading about a topic like domestic violence doesn't promote abusing a family member any more than reading about professional hockey promotes trying out for a team. Knowledge is power. Middle school readers and writers who are ready to tackle such topics can gain knowledge about who they are and what they believe through the ideas they find in young adult books—and they can do it safely from a distance, through the heart and experience of the trusted writer.

We also provide a step-by-step lesson based on each key quality which spells out in detail how you might teach that quality using one of the mentor texts in its entirety or a passage from it. These lessons are easy to use and they're fun. Add them to your collection of trait-specific teaching materials. You may want to share them at grade-level meetings or with your teaching team.

Many teachers are using technology to make teaching and learning more interesting and appealing. So, in the lessons, you'll notice references to electronic whiteboard projectors and electronic document cameras. If you have access to these tools, by all means, use them! But if you don't, fear not. The lessons can be carried out in the traditional manner. After all, it's hard to beat simply reading a fine passage to students and discussing it. Strong writing has always had the ability to get and hold our attention, no matter how we share it.

We hope this resource will inspire you to look at your library with new eyes: trait eyes. Learning to see the traits in great literature becomes second nature over time—and so does teaching writing using that literature, as you will discover. It is not only effective, but also a lot of fun. Let's get started.

CHAPTER I

Ideas

❝Really good writers can imagine all kind of things *to do with text*, and this imagination comes from their sense of craft, a sense garnered over time from reading like writers and from writing themselves—trying out the crafts they have come to understand.**❞**

—KATIE WOOD RAY from *Wondrous Words: Writers and Writing in the Elementary Classroom*

Imagining what is possible is what writers do with the ideas trait. From Philip Pullman, author of *The Golden Compass*, a young adult fantasy novel about new worlds and personal demons, to Sara Hoagland Hunter, author of *The Unbreakable Code*, a picture-book memoir about the Navajo "code breakers" and their role in WWII, the writers in this section explore a range of ideas and express them in a way that intrigues and informs the reader. Your students may have read fantasy novels before, but *The Golden Compass* takes them someplace fantastically new and different. They may have read memoirs before, but *The Unbreakable Code* is a unique story, based on an amazing, little-known historical event. Pullman, Hunter, and the other authors covered in this chapter use facts as well as their imaginations to create books with ideas that are fresh.

The ideas trait is about how writers use their imaginations to explore the unknown and use what they discover to make meaning for the reader. It is the piece's content—its central message and the details that support that message. The piece shows strength in the ideas trait when its topic is narrow and clear and its details are specific, interesting, and accurate. It is focused and well developed and contains original thinking, because the writer knows what he or she wants to say and anticipates the reader's every question. To accomplish this, the writer must apply the key qualities of this trait with skill and confidence:

* **Finding a Topic**

    The writer offers a clear central theme or a simple, original story line that is memorable.

* **Focusing the Topic**

    The writer narrows the theme or story line to create a piece that is clear, tight, and manageable.

* **Developing the Topic**

    The writer provides enough critical evidence to support the theme and shows insight on the topic. He or she tells the story in a fresh way through an original, unpredictable plot.

* **Using Details**

    The writer offers credible, accurate details that create pictures in the reader's mind, from the beginning of the piece to the end. Those details provide the reader with evidence of the writer's knowledge about and/or experience with the topic.

We've found that when middle school students cry out "I don't know what to write about," they're not telling the truth. They usually have a least a nugget of an idea. So what they really mean, we suspect, is they don't know how to handle the idea with the skill necessary to create a piece of writing that is fresh. They worry that anything they have to say won't be interesting. They are not alone. Every writer faces this fear every time he or she sits down to write.

By studying how the ideas trait works in mentor texts, students find inspiration in what other writers have done well and, in turn, learn techniques they might never have thought about trying. Just as Dorothy gave courage to the Scarecrow, these mentor texts give courage to writers. With courage comes a great question, "What should I do to make my idea mean something to the reader?" To answer that, students should turn to the key qualities of the ideas trait and ask, "How do I make my writing clear?" "Should I add more details or leave a few to the reader's imagination?" "Have I focused my topic or am I trying to do too much?" "Have I used my imagination to address this familiar topic in a whole new way?" The answers just might lie in one of the mentor texts recommended in this chapter.

Mentor Texts in This Chapter

Finding a Topic

Peppe the Lamplighter, Bartone

Pop's Bridge, Bunting

No More Dead Dogs, Korman

The Graveyard Book, Gaiman

Rain Is Not My Indian Name, Smith

The Greatest: Muhammad Ali, Myers

Focusing the Topic

Henry's Freedom Box, Levine

The Composition, Skármeta

Stanford Wong Flunks Big Time, Yee

The Golden Compass, Pullman

Suite Scarlett, Johnson

Chains, Anderson

Developing the Topic

The Orange Shoes, Noble

Knut: How One Little Polar Bear Captivated the World, Hatkoff, Hatkoff, Hatkoff & Ulich

Becoming Joe DiMaggio, Testa

Lupita Mañana, Beatty

Cracker! The Best Dog in Vietnam, Kadohata

Shiver, Stiefvater

Using Details

The Unbreakable Code, Hunter

An Angel for Solomon Singer, Rylant

Tangerine, Bloor

The House on Mango Street, Cisneros

Squashed, Bauer

Jack's Black Book, Gantos

Key Quality: Finding a Topic

Peppe the Lamplighter
Elisa Bartone
Ted Lewin, illustrator
Lothrop, Lee & Shepard Books, 1993

It is turn-of-the-century New York City, a place where people from all over the world are arriving daily in search of a better life. Peppe lives in a tenement with his father and seven sisters. To earn money, he lights Little Italy's streetlamps at dusk each night. Although Peppe is happy, his father is ashamed because such menial work is not what he envisioned for his only son when they left their Italian homeland. It is a disgrace. That is, until Peppe brings a near tragedy to a standstill while on duty. This is an inspiring story, based in part on an episode in the author's family history—when her grandfather immigrated to America from Italy. Encourage students to mine their family history for writing topics by talking to parents, grandparents, and other loved ones. They're guaranteed to strike gold.

Pop's Bridge
Eve Bunting
C. F. Payne, illustrator
Harcourt, Inc., 2006

The construction of the Golden Gate Bridge is one of the greatest feats of structural engineering in our country's history. Although we have one man to thank, Joseph Strauss, for establishing the vision, we have many, many others to thank for turning that vision into reality—workers who risked their lives daily to bring to completion what many claimed to be impossible. This is the story of one of those workers, a "skywalker," told from the point of view of his young son, Robert. Eve Bunting captures masterfully all of Robert's feelings about his pop's work—his pride in the project's grandeur, his fear of its danger, and his joy on the day the bridge opens, in May 1937. She proves that when we look at our built environment with a writer's eye, topics emerge. Behind every street, tunnel, building, and bridge, there is a story waiting to be told.

No More Dead Dogs

Gordon Korman
Hyperion, 2002

FOCUS LESSON: Page 25 When Wallace Wallace (his real name) claims that any award-winning book with a picture of a dog on its cover is sure to end with the death of the dog, his eighth-grade teacher, Mr. Fogelman, is offended. Wallace and his classmates have already suffered through *Sounder* in sixth grade and *Old Yeller* in seventh, and now it appears eighth grade will begin with another dead-dog story, *Old Shep, My Pal*. So, while in detention, Wallace produces a stage version of *Old Shep*; he makes some innovative changes to the book that include adding roller skates, rock music, and the dramatic recovery of a very ill Old Shep. In the end, Mr. Fogelman comes around to seeing things Wallace's way, and the school production of the play is a big hit. Gordon Korman once again succeeds in piquing the reader's interest in the topic of school life through capturing its hallmarks: boring books, boring plays, biased teachers, and rebels without causes.

The Graveyard Book

Neil Gaiman
HarperCollins, 2008

A sinister, dark figure, known only as "the man Jack," has, for some mysterious reason, come to kill 18-month-old Bod in the middle of the night. But the boy escapes to a nearby graveyard, where he spends the next thirteen years under the care and guidance of his adoptive ghost parents: Mr. and Mrs. Owens, who died during Victorian times; a werewolf nanny; a personal guardian, who may be a vampire; and other assorted unearthly residents. Each chapter takes Bod through a new adventure, including a dangerous trip to the world of ghouls, a confrontation with bullies at school, and a friendship outside the cemetery that brings the story full circle. Neil Gaiman's modern fairy tale, a Newbery Medal winner, is funny, scary, and charming. With the introduction of each new character, Gaiman faithfully suggests that people (and creatures) are not good or evil because of what they are, but because of what they do.

Questions to Ask When Choosing Books

When browsing the bookstore or library for books to use when teaching about ideas, ask yourself:

- Is the book on a topic I like? A topic my students like? A theme I want to cover? Does it help to meet content standards I have to cover?

- Does the author care about the topic and have something new to say about it? Does he or she zero in on a small part of a big idea?

- Has the author thought deeply about what my students need to know? Is the content convincing, interesting, and accurate?

- Will the writing create pictures in my students' minds? Do details draw upon the five senses? Do they support the book's main topic? Are they original?

Rain Is Not My Indian Name

Cynthia Leitich Smith
HarperCollins, 2001

Life seems to keep handing Cassidy Rain Bergoff more hardship than the average person should receive. Just as she and her friend, Galen, are becoming more than friends, he is killed in a traffic accident, flooding Rain with memories of her mother's death and leaving her with more grief than she can bear. Despite the fact that they love her, her remaining family members don't provide much help, and Rain retreats from the world. Although she is of mixed heritage (Cherokee/Creek/Ojibway/Scots Irish/German), she has never been interested in anything related to her Native American roots, especially her Aunt Georgia's annual Indian Camp, where young people learn about the culture of their indigenous nation. When Rain is assigned to photograph the camp for the local paper, she becomes curious. And when federal funding for the camp is threatened, she becomes passionately involved. Smith uses her protagonist's dialogue, actions, and inner conflict to generate the novel's topic: searching for personal identity despite a whirlwind of life events.

The Greatest: Muhammad Ali

Walter Dean Myers
Scholastic, 2001

As no other author has, Walter Dean Myers captures the life of one of the world's most celebrated and influential men—the man *Sports Illustrated* named the "Greatest Athlete of the twentieth Century"—Muhammad Ali. From the Grace Community Center in Louisville, Kentucky, where a young Cassius Clay first learned "the sweet science" of boxing, to the 1996 Atlanta Olympics, where a fifty-four-year-old Ali, suffering from Parkinson's Disease, trembled as he lit the Olympic Flame, Myers illuminates Ali's entire life. A contemporary of Ali, he points out that Ali stood as the representative of all African Americans in ways no one else ever had. As such, this is as much a story of the struggle for civil rights as it is of Ali. Myers attributes Ali's boxing success to courage, intelligence, and hard work, without making excuses for his mistakes in life. Myers includes both sides of this story about a man who rose from poverty to inspire a nation to change, even during times when his personal life betrayed him. For nonfiction, this book reads like magic. (Mature Themes)

Key Quality: Focusing the Topic

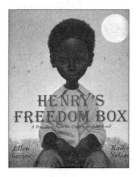

Henry's Freedom Box

Ellen Levine
Kadir Nelson, illustrator
Scholastic, 2007

Henry Brown is one of about four million slaves living in the United States in the mid-1800s. When he loses what matters to him most—his wife and children—and comes to feel he has little to lose in risking his life for freedom, he makes a desperate move. He asks a white abolitionist to pack him in a crate and mail him from Richmond, Virginia, to freedom in Philadelphia, Pennsylvania. The journey by train and steamboat is grueling, as Henry is shifted and stacked like the rest of the cargo. But he survives. And although nothing can erase the crimes carried out against him, he is a free man. He has hope. This is an excellent example of how writers often take a big event, such as slavery just before the Civil War, and extract one story from it to make a powerful statement.

The Composition

Antonio Skármeta
Alfonso Ruano, illustrator
Groundwood Books, 2000

FOCUS LESSON: Page 26 Pedro is like most nine-year-old boys. He goes to school, plays soccer, and enjoys spending time with his friends and family. But unlike most nine-year-old boys, he lives in a country ruled by a dictator. Pedro's parents do their best to shield their son from that fact, while quietly keeping informed about political matters. But when Pedro witnesses his best friend's father being arrested for mysterious reasons, he knows something's terribly wrong. The next day, government officials go to Pedro's school and give the children a writing assignment: They must describe their parents' daily activities—what they read, watch, discuss, and so forth. Pedro realizes that telling the truth will lead to disaster, so he writes about imaginary, harmless activities. Skármeta exposes a curious fact about writing—that what we withhold can be as just as potent as what we divulge.

Stanford Wong Flunks Big-Time

Lisa Yee
Scholastic, 2005

On the last day of sixth grade, Stanford Wong finds his dreams of seventh-grade basketball stardom will come crashing down if he doesn't do something over the summer to bring up an "F" in English. Enter girl genius and English tutor, Millicent Min. Stanford thinks Millicent is totally uncool—in his words, a "poster girl for Chinese geekdom." Millicent is as irritated by the arrangement as

Stanford, if not more so. But as the two work together over the summer, a friendship is forged over the fire of things they have in common. As a result, Stanford grows in surprising ways. Lisa Yee captures teenage society perfectly through an assortment of evolving young characters, especially Stanford and Millicent. Yee focuses her main idea through dialogue and conflict, showing that teens lead complicated lives, often balancing personal hopes and dreams with family and cultural expectations.

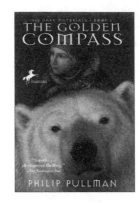

The Golden Compass

Philip Pullman
Scholastic, 1995

Eleven-year-old Lyra Belacqua, who has the run of the fictional Jordan College at Oxford University, leaves England and sets out to solve the mystery of the Gobblers, a secret society rumored to be stealing children and whisking them away to the far north. On the way, she is rescued from abductors by the Gyptians, with whom she teams up. She also hires an armored, mercenary polar bear. When Lyra reaches the northern city of Bolvangar, she finds that something horrible is being done to the kidnapped children and, to make matters worse, she discovers that her mother and father are involved. Lyra's polar-bear friend, a legion of avenging witches, and the Gyptians will save the day, but not before Lyra learns the truth about her mother and father and the potential holocaust they are preparing. Pullman narrows the focus of his story from fantasy adventure to spiritual allegory (the isolation of the human spirit) by moving setting and characters from the fairly familiar to the totally and delightfully exotic.

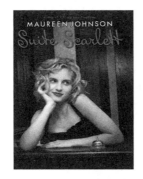

Suite Scarlett

Maureen Johnson
Scholastic, 2008

When Mrs. Amy Amberson, an eccentric, aging actress, checks into the Empire Suite of the decaying Hopewell Hotel, it becomes Scarlett Martin's responsibility to look after her. Business has taken a downward turn for the Martin family, proprietors of the hotel, and the only remaining staff is composed of family members, who must take pains to keep guests content. Mrs. Amberson is a bit of a pain herself, albeit a lovable one, and she has Scarlett hopping all summer carrying out her crazy ideas, which, for better or worse, include trying to save a production of her brother's play. Along the way, Scarlett mends her relationship with her sisters and develops a crush on one of the play's actors. Maureen Johnson has a wonderful wit, as proven in the book's sharp, very authentic dialogue. By telling the story through the protagonist's eyes, Johnson focuses the theme, allowing Scarlett's perception of people and events to lead the reader through the story.

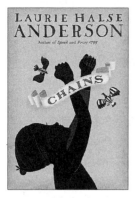

Chains
Laurie Halse Anderson
Simon & Schuster, 2008

As the storm of the American Revolutionary War brews, New York City is a central location in the struggle among the Patriots (the colonists) and the Loyalists (the British and their sympathizers). When Isabel and Ruth are sold to a cruel Loyalist family, the Locktons, they find themselves powerless over their own fate, but not so over the fate of the nation. At thirteen, Isabel becomes a spy for the Patriot army and helps derail an assassination attempt on George Washington, among other Loyalist plots. Anderson conducted comprehensive research to make this book as accurate as possible. As a result, readers will be surprised and horrified by many of the facts she presents—from the brand burned into Isabel's face, marking her a slave, to the denial of personhood she suffers, even at the hands of the Patriots whose very lives she is saving. Anderson maintains her focus on the injustice of slavery by repeatedly raising Isabel's, and the reader's, hopes that freedom is minutes away, only to dash those hopes again and again.

Key Quality: Developing the Topic

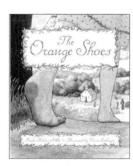

The Orange Shoes
Trinka Hakes Noble
Doris Ettlinger, illustrator
Sleeping Bear Press, 2007

Being poor doesn't really bother Delly Porter because, as far as she's concerned, she has everything that matters—a loving family, a nightly meal, a homemade sketchbook, and a kind teacher, Miss Violet. Each day, she walks to school shoeless, enjoying the feel of smooth dirt under her feet. That is, until Prudy Winfield, a classmate with no heart and more shoes than she needs, ridicules Delly for going barefoot. And then, to make matters worse, Prudy destroys the new orange shoes that Delly's father buys her for the forthcoming Shoebox Social, a school fundraiser. Delly's faith is nearly destroyed, too, until she figures out a way to use her artistic skills and winning personality to raise more money at the Shoebox Social than she ever could have dreamed. Noble takes the topic of bullying and develops it into story that will move every reader.

Knut: How One Little Polar Bear Captivated the World
Juliana, Isabella, and Craig Hatkoff, and Dr. Gerald R. Uhlich
Scholastic, 2007

The authors of the bestselling *Owen & Mzee* bring us this true-life tale of one man's devotion to an orphaned polar bear cub. The story unfolds gently, starting with Knut's birth at Zoo Berlin, then moving onto his mother's abandonment, his brother's death, and bearkeeper Thomas Dörflein's decision to assume the role of foster father and provide round-the-clock care. The authors describe eloquently the lengths to which Thomas went to ensure Knut's survival—creating the perfect climate-controlled environment, feeding him just the right food, and even strumming Elvis tunes for him on the guitar. Because of Thomas's efforts, Knut does more than survive. He thrives. And when he makes his first public appearance, both he and Thomas receive a hero's welcome. Hats off to the Hatskoffs for exploring their topic so thoroughly!

Becoming Joe DiMaggio
Maria Testa
Candlewick, 2002

It is the first half of the twentieth century, and there's no activity Joseph and his grandfather, Papa-Angelo, enjoy more together than sidling up to the radio and listening to New York Yankees baseball games. Fellow Italian, Joe DiMaggio, is their hero. In fact, Joseph was named for him. He is certainly not named for his father, a man who physically abuses his wife, spends time in prison, and dodges the draft during World War II. In this collection of 24 free-verse poems, Joe's life story unfolds. The poems focus on major events of the time—both historical, such as President Roosevelt's battle cry, "We have nothing to fear but fear itself," the attack on Pearl Harbor, the arrival of V-J Day, and Joe DiMaggio's 56-homerun summer, and personal, such as the tomatoes and peppers that Joe's grandfather brings as an expression of love and the revelation that young Joe will become a doctor. The power and influence of Joe and his grandfather's loving relationship are developed through the one constant that remains despite war, family problems, and economic crisis: listening together to baseball games on the radio.

Lupita Mañana
Patricia Beatty
HarperCollins, 1981

When Señora Torres is widowed, she cannot support herself and her six children in their hometown of Ensenada, Mexico. So her two oldest children, Lupita and Salvador, seek work across the border in Indio, California, where their Aunt Consuelo lives as an American citizen. Crossing the border proves both difficult and dangerous. Once they arrive in Indio and find work as dishwashers and vegetable harvesters, Lupita and Salvador live in constant fear of *la migra*, the immigration police. But they earn enough money to pay off the loan that provides food and shelter for their family in Mexico. Life becomes more complicated, however, when Salvador threatens to turn his back on his family, while Lupita continues to work. Beatty captures the complexities of immigration, especially for teenagers, through Lupita's evolving relationship with her brother, members of her extended family, and her new environment.

Cracker! The Best Dog in Vietnam
Cynthia Kadohata
Atheneum, 2007

FOCUS LESSON: Page 28 Rick Hanski is a hard-headed seventeen-year-old private in the Vietnam War, with several write-ups for fighting. He signs up to be a dog handler and winds up with Cracker, a German shepherd that shows little promise of being trained. However, after a rocky start, Cracker and Rick become a great team. They lead patrols, searching out booby traps and snipers. They go on a mission to rescue American prisoners of war. In the process, Cracker and Rick grow closer. When Rick is wounded in an ambush, Cracker is lost in the jungle. Rick winds up back in the States, saddened by the loss of the one thing he cares about most in the world. Cracker is just as devoted to Rick—so much, in fact, that she makes her way through miles of jungle to American soldiers. From there, Cracker and Rick are reunited. This is a meticulously researched, carefully developed story. Kadohata develops her story's main idea, the vulnerability of soldiers (including dogs), by constantly putting her characters in harm's way and allowing their interdependency to come to the surface.

Shiver

Maggie Stiefvater
Scholastic, 2009

Grace, an independent seventeen-year-old, was only nine when something happened that changed the course of her life. While wandering the woods behind her house, a wolf pack attacked her, but surprisingly one member saved her, the one with the yellow eyes she never forgets. Grace spends hours staring into the woods, hoping to catch a glimpse of them again. When she sees the wolf staring out at her, she goes to him, unafraid, hand outstretched, hoping to coax him closer. But he always shies away. The story develops when it shifts from Grace's point of view to 18-year-old Sam's. Sam has loved Grace from afar for years. When local boy Jack is killed by the wolf pack, the townspeople band together to hunt down the vicious animals once and for all. During the hunt, Sam is shot, but manages to crawl to Grace's back yard, naked and bleeding. Grace recognizes immediately that he is her wolf—the eyes give him away. Sam's resistance to change back into wolf form becomes the story's driving force. Grace's realization that Sam was the wolf who saved her life compels her to return his love. Together, they fight to sustain his human form. Stiefvater is masterful at walking a thin line between fantasy and chilling reality. (Mature Themes)

Key Quality: Using Details

The Unbreakable Code

Sara Hoagland Hunter
Julia Miner, illustrator
Rising Moon, 1996

This book pays homage to the Navajo "code talkers" of World War II—a little-known group of about 420 soldiers who served in the Marine Corps. Their job? To send and receive critical radio messages using a code created from the Navajo language. Since that language had never been transcribed and was unknown to outsiders, the Japanese could not intercept the messages. Hunter tells this detail-rich story through a former code talker—the grandfather of John, a boy who is on the verge of leaving his beloved canyon home for a new life in Minnesota with his mother and stepfather. To reassure John, his grandfather tells him about his past—how he once left the canyon to serve his country—but returned, just as John will do one day. As part of her research, Hunter interviewed actual code talkers, which explains why her details are so vivid and convincing.

An Angel for Solomon Singer

Cynthia Rylant
Peter Catalanotto, illustrator
Scholastic, 1992

Nobody uses details like Cynthia Rylant. Nobody. In her amusing
chapter-book series, such as Mr. Putter and Tabby, and award-winning
novels, such as *Missing May*, you'll find them—rich details derived
from what her characters see, hear, smell, touch, and taste. Her picture
books are no exception. *An Angel for Solomon Singer* is the story
of a lonely man who lives in a grim hotel for men in New York City. To escape, he walks
the streets and dreams about someday returning to his Indiana home. One evening, those
dreams draw him into the Westway Cafe, where he meets a waiter who restores his hope
with nothing more than a comforting smile and a few kind words. Night after night, on the
waiter's encouragement, the man returns to the cafe—and with each visit, he grows stronger,
happier, and more fulfilled. As the saying goes, God is in the details.

Tangerine

Edward Bloor
Harcourt, Inc., 1997

Paul Fisher is a second-class citizen in his own home. His parents
lavish their attention on his older brother, Erik, a football player,
and practically ignore Paul, a soccer player, which is criminal
considering that Paul is nearly blind. Although his vision has been
corrected with Coke-bottle glasses, he can't quite remember how
he suffered his loss of eyesight in the first place. Something is not
right with this family. There are secrets. But secrets often have a
way of coming out into the light. Erik will get what he deserves, and Paul's suppressed
memories will be revealed. This is an artistically written book that touches upon some
common ills in American society. Bloor obscures some details while meticulously describing
others to keep the reader moving through the story.

The House on Mango Street

Sandra Cisneros
Vintage, 1981

FOCUS LESSON: Page 30 In this somewhat autobiographical set of 44 short pieces
describing a Mexican-American family's experiences in
Chicago, Sandra Cisneros delicately opens the mind and heart of
Esperanza, a young girl moving through her teen years. A bigoted
teacher, an insensitive friend, sexually criminal boys and men—all
of these people and others ambush the initially innocent Esperanza,
whose pain rises right up through the page. At the same time,
life-chronicling events and family traditions are given equal attention and are described in
lively, loving detail. As the stories progress, Esperanza transforms from a little girl to a young

woman. She sees the causes and effects of sexism and racism in her society and seeks ways to overcome them. Readers will be amazed at how deeply a young woman can reflect on the reality of her world. Cisneros's details put the reader inside the experience.

Squashed
Joan Bauer
Delacorte, 1992

Pumpkin growing is serious business in Rock River, Iowa, and Ellie Morgan is hoping to prove herself a champion at the upcoming state fair with her pride and joy, Max, a 600-plus pounder. Ellie may be obsessed with the pumpkin-growing contest, but for good reason. She may be using it as a way to process the grief she feels over the death of her mother. As the fair grows closer, additional issues complicate Ellie's life: a love interest, pumpkin thieves, struggles with weight loss, unpredictable Iowa weather, a mean-spirited competitor, and more. Readers will find themselves cheering for Ellie, who will kiss and be kissed, begin to accept the loss of her mother, and come home from the fair with a blue ribbon. Bauer is a master of detail.

Jack's Black Book
Jack Gantos
Farrar, Straus and Giroux, 1999

Nothing ever seems to go right for thirteen-year-old Jack Henry, the autobiographical stand-in for the author Jack Gantos, who simply cannot get a break. His dog digs a hole, but breaks his neck falling into it. Jack builds him a coffin in industrial arts class, but must dig up the interred remains of the poor pup to use it. While their parents are gone, Jack and his sister, Betsy, nearly set the baby on fire. Although he is committed to becoming a writer, an IQ test tells him he doesn't have the intelligence for anything but physical work. In addition to Jack's own personality quirks, those of his family members, friends, and teachers are woven into the story. Each vignette is told in gross, gory detail, which will have middle school boys rolling on the floor in laughter.

Focus Lesson 1: Finding a Topic

CHAPTER BOOK

No More Dead Dogs
Gordon Korman

Think About the Writer's Work:

- Did he choose a topic he seems to like?

- Does he have something new to say about this topic?

- Is he writing about what he seems to know and care about?

- Has he gathered enough information so he's got plenty to write about?

Lesson Focus:

Wallace Wallace, eighth-grade football hero, is tired of reading books in which the dog dies, and he says as much in his review of *Old Shep, My Pal*. Unfortunately, his English teacher, Mr. Fogelman, takes exception to his opinion, gives Wallace a detention, and insists that he rewrite the review. But Wallace won't budge, which ultimately costs him his position on the team. Ironically, Wallace learns a valuable lesson about friendship not from the members of the football team, but from students in the school play. Mr. Fogelman's adaptation of *Old Shep, My Pal*. In this lesson, students explore different ways to write about dogs... living or dead!

Materials:

- a copy of *No More Dead Dogs*

- projection and copies of the Think About the Writer's Work questions above

- access to the Internet

- paper, pens, pencils

- projection of the following passage from Chapter 1, "Enter Wallace Wallace":

> "I wasn't surprised," I said. "I knew Old Shep was going to die before I started page one."
>
> "Don't be ridiculous," the teacher snapped. "How?"
>
> I shrugged. "Because the dog always dies. Go to the library and pick out a book with an award sticker and a dog on the cover. Trust me, that dog is going down."

What to Do:

1. Summarize the plot of *No More Dead Dogs* for students. Ask them to look up other plot summaries by going to Amazon.com, Barnesandnoble.com, Borders.com, Powells.com, and other virtual bookstores, as well as library Web sites. Have students print out the summaries and compare them.

2. Tell students that one of the book's themes is that the main character, Wallace Wallace, is tired of reading award-winning books in which a dog dies, including *Old Shep, My Pal*.

3. Ask students to brainstorm actual award-winning books in which a dog dies, such as *Old Yeller, Where the Red Fern Grows*, and *Sounder*, and create a classroom list of titles. If they wish, have them search the Internet for more books to add to their list.

4. Go to the library and gather as many of the books from their list as possible. For books that aren't available in the library, invite students to download plot summaries from the Internet.

5. Put students in groups of two to three, assign each group a book, and ask members to familiarize themselves with it by reading the jacket copy or the Internet plot summary.

6. Ask groups to change the plot so the dog does not die and write a new summary. Have them include as many details as necessary to make their new plot credible and interesting to the reader. Remind them to refer to the Think About the Writer's Work questions as they write.

7. Have a representative from each group share the original plots and the new plots with the class and discuss.

Lesson Extension:

Ask students to think about Wallace Wallace's disagreement with his English teacher. Create a panel made up of eight students, half of whom sympathize with Wallace Wallace and half of whom do not. Then have members debate whether Wallace was right to write the book review to reflect what he honestly thought and felt, or if he should have written the review the teacher asked for. Ask the class to weigh in about how Wallace Wallace dealt with his problem and how far each of them would go to stand on a principle that reflected his or her own values.

Focus Lesson 2: Focusing the Topic

PICTURE BOOK

The Composition
Antonio Skármeta

Think About the Writer's Work:

• Has he zeroed in on one small part of a bigger idea?

• Can the idea be retold in a simple sentence?

• Has he chosen the information that best captures the idea?

• Has he thought deeply about what the reader will need to know?

Lesson Focus:

Pedro is a soccer-loving boy living in a country ruled by a dictator. Life is peaceful for Pedro until he witnesses a friend's father being arrested for some mysterious crime against the government. Pedro worries that what happened to Daniel's father will happen to his parents.

When officers ask students to enter a "contest" to write a composition about what their families do at night, Pedro realizes he can't tell the truth if he is to protect the people he loves. In this lesson, students discover the focus of the book by guessing its main idea while listening to it being read aloud.

Materials:

- a copy of *The Composition*

- projection and copies of the Think About the Writer's Work questions above

- projections of selected illustrations and passages from the book

- paper, pens, pencils

What to Do:

1. Explain to students that you are going to read a picture book to them that has a very focused topic and that you will help them discover that topic as the story unfolds.

2. Share the Think About the Writer's Work questions and discuss the importance of having a focused topic when writing, rather than a broad one.

3. Make sure students have an understanding of the difference between a democracy and a dictatorship. Ask them to discuss the differences between the two forms of government. A democracy is a government of and by the people, where representatives of the people, chosen through elections, make the decisions. A dictatorship is a government in which there is a centralization of power that all rests with one person.

4. Begin reading *The Composition* to students and stop at the end of the page that says, "'I'm little, but I'm smart and fast. The only thing that's fast about you guys is your mouth,' Pedro retorted." Make sure students see the words and pictures by using a document camera or facing the pages toward students as you read.

5. Ask students to jot down the main idea of the story. They may decide it's Pedro and his excellent soccer skills, or perhaps his feelings about being smaller than other kids. Remind students to use the Think About the Writer's Work questions to help them decide.

6. Read to students the line that says, "A neighbor came up and ran his hand through Daniel's hair. 'I'll help you close up,' he said." Ask students if they've changed their minds about the story's main idea. If they have, ask them to write down their new thoughts. For example, they may add that the story's focus is about what happens to people who oppose the government.

7. Read to students the line that says, "'Go to bed, son,' said his father." Ask students how they're feeling about the story's main idea and if your third reading changed their minds about it. Have them write down any new thoughts. They may note that the focused topic is about the different responsibilities of adults and children.

8. Finish reading the book. Ask students to write down what they believe the focused topic is now that they've read the different details that develop throughout the story. They will likely realize that it is the difficult decision Pedro makes to lie in his composition to protect his family.

Focus Lesson

9. Review the Think About the Writer's Work questions with students, noting how Skármeta uses details to focus his topic. Make a list of the details from the story that supports the focused topic.

Lesson Extension:

Ask students why the book ends with Pedro's father saying, "We'd better buy a chess set." Discuss other ways the family might protect itself from the government.

Focus Lesson 3: Developing the Topic

YOUNG ADULT NOVEL

Cracker! The Best Dog in Vietnam
Cynthia Kadohata

Think About the Writer's Work:

- Is the information correct?
- Are the details chock-full of interesting information?
- Has she used details that show new thinking about this idea?
- Will the reader believe what she says about this topic?

Lesson Focus:

Set during the Vietnam War and told from the point-of-view of Cracker, a German Shepherd, and her handler, Rick, this realistic novel focuses on the military program in which dogs are trained to sniff out explosives, track down POWs, and carry out other important missions during times of war. The book's topic develops as readers get insider perspective on how Cracker and Rick work together in missions to save fellow soldiers time and time again. In this lesson, students read a passage from Rick's point-of-view and retell it in writing from Cracker's to show how the topic develops by filling in thoughts and feelings.

Materials:

- a copy of *Cracker! The Best Dog in Vietnam*
- projection and copies of the Think About the Writer's Work questions above
- paper, pens, pencils
- projection of the following passage from Chapter 14:

> Her ears flickered again, and again Rick debated halting everybody. But Cracker kept walking, so he kept walking. This was so different from training. Now he had to interpret Cracker even more exactly, had to understand precisely what each flick of her ears meant. Otherwise, if he stopped the company too often, they might think he was crying wolf and not take Cracker seriously. And if he didn't stop the company when there was real danger, men might die. He felt sick to his stomach.

What to Do:

1. Give students an overview of *Cracker!* and tell them you are going to share a passage from it with them.

2. Share the Think About the Writer's Work questions and review them with students. Explain that when writers develop the body of a piece, whether it is fiction or nonfiction, they need to decide how much information to include and how best to reveal that information. Exploring the different points of view of characters within the story can both develop the topic and make the writing interesting.

3. Project the passage above, read it, and ask students what they learned about the use of dogs in the military to track down explosives such as land mines and keep the soldiers as safe as possible.

4. Challenge students to rewrite the passage from Cracker's point of view. Tell them they must convey information that develops the story, but this time through the perspective of the dog, not his handler. Ask them to consider details that the dog would include that the handler might not, such as what the dog hopes the handler will understand by flattening his ears.

5. When students have finished, invite a few of them to share their revisions with the class. Review the Think About the Writer's Work questions again with the class to help students judge which pieces are the most effective. Which are the most believable? Which contain the clearest information? Which contain the strongest details? Which develop the body of the story most effectively?

6. If time allows, ask students to revise the passage again, only this time from the point of view of a soldier other than Rick or one of the other major characters in the book, taking care to add different details and observations that this character would find important.

Lesson Extension:

Ask students to find a passage from a favorite fiction book and retell it from the point of view of one of the other characters. Tell them that what is said would remain the same but the details and explanations would vary depending on the character they pick. Encourage students to add information as necessary to make the writing clear as the main idea is developed.

YOUNG ADULT NOVEL

Focus Lesson 4: Using Details

The House on Mango Street
Sandra Cisneros

Think About the Writer's Work:

- Did she create a picture in the reader's mind?

- Did she use details that draw upon the five senses (sight, touch, taste, smell, hearing)?

- Do her details stay on the main topic?

- Did she stretch for details beyond the obvious?

Lesson Focus:

Esperanza Cordero is a young girl growing up in the Latino section of Chicago. Her world is chaotic and harsh, and Esperanza desperately wants to escape it. The reader comes to know Esperanza, laughing, crying, and feeling all the emotions she experiences, because of Cisneros's detailed and evocative prose. In this lesson, students examine a passage from the book that describes the main character's laugh and then write short pieces about different kinds of laughs such as a chuckles, giggles, and guffaws, using rich details.

Materials:

- a copy of *The House on Mango Street*

- projection and copies of the Think About the Writer's Work questions above

- paper, pens, pencils

- old magazines, scissors, glue, tape, 8½-by-11-inch pieces of posterboard

- projection of the following passage from the vignette entitled "Laughter":

> Nenny and I don't look like sisters… not right away. Not the way you can tell with Rachel and Lucy, who have the same fat popsicle lips like everybody else in their family. But me and Nenny, we are more alike than you would know. Our laughter, for example. Not the shy ice cream bells' giggle of Rachel and Lucy's family, but all of a sudden and surprised like a pile of dishes breaking.

What to Do:

1. Summarize *The House on Mango Street* for students and explain that the book is written in short, self-contained vignettes that add up to a rich portrait of the main character, Esperanza Cordero.

2. Discuss the fact that family members both in the book and in real life often have similar mannerisms, such as furrowing their eyes when they are angry, using their hands when they talk, and running their fingers through their hair when they are exasperated. Ask students to share any mannerisms that they have in common with other family members.

Ideas

3. Explain that in the vignette "Laughter," Cisneros describes the similar-sounding laughs of Esperanza and her sister Nenny. Read the passage that appears on page 30.

4. Show students the Think About the Writer's Work questions for this lesson and the passage, and read the passage again. Ask students to tell you which details stand out most and why. Encourage them to be specific by using the Think About the Writer's Work questions. Underline the details that students identify.

5. Ask students if anyone thinks their laugh sounds like Esperanza's. Discuss the difference between a "shy ice cream bell giggle" and one that is "all of a sudden and surprised and sounds like a pile of dishes breaking."

6. Brainstorm types of laughs and write them on a whiteboard: guffaws, bellows, titters, snorts, chuckles, belly laughs, and so on.

7. Assign pairs of students to the different types of laughs and ask them to write a paragraph that describes it so clearly that readers will recognize it immediately.

8. When they've finished, ask for volunteers to read their paragraphs and see if other students can identify the laugh.

9. Have students cut out the letters in their laugh's name from old magazines and glue them to the top of the posterboard to create a title. Then have them glue their laugh descriptions to the posterboard. Encourage them to illustrate their posters to give the posters interest and make them unique.

10. Hang the posters around the room for all to enjoy.

Lesson Extension:

Read aloud other passages from *The House on Mango Street* and discuss Cisneros's vivid details that describe the characters, setting, and feelings. Encourage students to revise a piece of their own writing by adding details, using the Think About the Writer's Work questions to guide them.

CHAPTER 2

Organization

"Reading well precedes writing well. Of all the ancestors claimed by a fine piece of prose, the most important is the prose from which the writer learned his craft. Writers learn craft not by memorizing rules about restrictive clauses, but by striving to equal a standard formed from reading."

—DONALD HALL and D. L. EMBLEN from
A Writer's Reader, Seventh Edition

A big part of writing well means being able to organize ideas logically and effectively from the beginning of the piece to the end—one of the most challenging skills for young writers to master. By reading well-organized books, students discover methods for beginning, ending, and structuring their own writing. Books such as *Holes,* by Louis Sachar, that captivate readers from the first line. Or books such as *American Born Chinese,* a graphic novel in which Gene Luen Yang presents three separate stories that come together seamlessly. Or books such as *Lily Quench and the Black Mountains,* by Natalie Jane Prior, that contain endings that leave readers sated yet hungry for more. These books create a standard for organizing text which students can aspire to and meet.

Organization is the internal structure of the piece—the thread of meaning, the pattern of logic. Typical structures include point-by-point analysis, chronological play of events, deductive logic, cause and effect, comparison and contrast, problem and solution, and order of importance and complexity. The structure the writer chooses depends on his or her purpose for writing and the intended audience.

Writing that is well organized unfolds sensibly. It starts with an introduction that creates a sense of anticipation for the reader. Events and information are presented in the right doses and at the right moments, so the reader never loses sight of the main idea. Transitions from one point to the next are strong. Well-organized writing closes with a sense of resolution; the writer ties up loose ends and answers important questions, while leaving the reader with a thing or two to ponder. To accomplish all this, the writer must skillfully and confidently apply the organization trait's key qualities:

✳ **Creating the Lead**
The writer grabs the reader's attention from the start and leads him or her into the piece naturally. He or she entices the reader, providing a tantalizing glimpse of what is to come.

✳ **Using Sequence Words and Transition Words**
The writer includes a variety of carefully selected sequence words (such as *later*, *then*, and *meanwhile*) and transition words (such as *however*, *also*, and *clearly*), which are placed wisely to guide the reader through the piece by showing how ideas progress, relate, and/or diverge.

✳ **Structuring the Body**
The writer creates a piece that is easy to follow, by fitting details together logically. He or she slows down to spotlight important points or events, and speeds up when he or she needs to move the reader along.

✳ **Ending With a Sense of Resolution**
The writer sums up his or her thinking in a natural, thoughtful, and convincing way. He or she anticipates and answers any lingering questions the reader may have, providing a strong sense of closure.

Students who are fed a steady diet of graphic organizers, or who are always told how many paragraphs their papers should have before they write a single word, will never become good organizers because they are not being given opportunities to push themselves and try out all the techniques available to them. This struggle is essential to the learning. Use the books in this section to ease their pain

Mentor Texts in This Chapter

Creating the Lead
Hannah's Journal, Moss

Gone Wild: An Endangered Animal Alphabet, McLimans

Holes, Sachar

The Dark Hills Divide, Carman

The Softwire: Virus on Orbis 1, Haarsma

Instead of Three Wishes, Turner

Using Sequence Words and Transition Words
Beautiful Warrior, McCully

The Journey: Stories of Migration, Rylant

A Year Down Yonder, Peck

The Westing Game, Raskin

My Father, the Angel of Death, Villareal

Forged by Fire, Draper

Structuring the Body
The Wall: Growing Up Behind the Iron Curtain, Sís

Meanwhile Back at the Ranch, Noble

Crossing Jordan, Fogelin

Pacific Crossing, Soto

American Born Chinese, Yang

Downriver, Hobbs

Ending With a Sense of Resolution
Rachel: The Story of Rachel Carson, Ehrlich

No! McPhail

Lily Quench and the Black Mountains, Prior

The Legend of Spud Murphy, Colfer

My Life in Dog Years, Paulsen

The Skin I'm In, Flake

Key Quality: Creating the Lead

Hannah's Journal: The Story of an Immigrant Girl

Marissa Moss, author and illustrator
Harcourt, Inc., 2000

With the Young American Voices series, students can immerse themselves in our nation's past by reading the journals of fictitious but quite believable girls from various historical periods. *Hannah's Journal* is the story of a ten-year-old girl who immigrates to America in 1901 to escape the growing persecution of Jews in Russia and to seek the education she's not allowed to receive there. Marissa Moss brings the journey alive by filling the book with drawings, photographs, and bits of ephemera such as a passport, a steamship ticket, and an inspection card. And the voice she creates for Hannah is right on target, right from the start: "Today is my birthday. I am now ten years old and Papashka gave me this journal to write in. All this paper just for me!" What ensues is a story that will delight, disturb, and inspire any child.

Gone Wild: An Endangered Animal Alphabet

David McLimans
Walker & Company, 2006

We know what you're asking: "An alphabet book for *middle school* students?" And our answer is an emphatic "Yes!" This is a rare alphabet book that will appeal to young folks, old folks, and everyone in between. David McLimans's illustrations are stunning—and his message is alarming. All of the animals depicted are critically endangered, endangered, or vulnerable. McLimans makes that clear by using powerful, inarguable statistics in his lead: "Our planet is home to so many plants and animals that it is impossible to know exactly how many species are sharing the earth with us. So far, scientists have named and described almost 1.5 million species, yet ninety percent of plants and invertebrates still haven't been identified. . . . There are more than 5,000 animals facing extinction." Share this book, ask students to pick social issues that matter to them, have them research related statistics, and write persuasive pieces.

Holes

Louis Sachar
Farrar, Straus and Giroux, 1998

Stanley Yelnats IV comes from a long line of Stanley Yelnatses, all of whom have suffered from a generations-old gypsy curse placed upon his "no-good-dirty-rotten-pig-stealing, great, great grandfather." As such, he is a friendless, hopeless, overweight introvert. Bad luck strikes again when Stanley is wrongly convicted of stealing a famous athlete's shoes and sent to Camp Green Lake, a detention center for boys, where the detainees dig holes every day, in service of a devious warden who wants the treasure rumored to be buried there. Although life seems to have gone from bad to worse, Stanley and his newfound friends experience good fortune when Stanley strikes a deal with a modern-day gypsy and the curse is lifted. Interwoven connections among characters create a fabric for an ingenious tale of bad luck turned good. Sachar's opening, a description of the dangers of Camp Green Lake, is so strong and intriguing, it will have readers rushing through the opening pages to discover how those dangers play out.

The Dark Hills Divide: The Land of Elyon, Book 1

Patrick Carman
Scholastic, 2005

In this first book of a three-book series, we are introduced to Elyon, a mystical land in which four cities, Bridewell, Lunenburg, Lathbury, and Turlock, are connected to each other and protected from the rest of Elyon by high walls. The terrors lurking outside the walls aren't entirely clear to twelve-year-old Alexa; all she knows is that there are "dangerous things" out there. As Warvold, the builder of the walls, is dying, he predicts to Alexa that secrets from both sides of the walls "are about to meet" and leaves her with the key to the outside. Alexa sets out on a quest in which she talks with people and animals and discovers the truth about the walls and their consequences. All in all, this fairy tale/fantasy/allegory is about what gets walled in when we attempt to wall things out, as well as the impact of human engineering on ecosystems. The story begins with Warvold hinting at the secrets outside Elyon's walls, passing on the golden key to the gate, and dying before he can explain, leaving the mystery for Alexa to solve.

The Softwire: Virus on Orbis 1

PJ Haarsma
Candlewick, 2006

FOCUS LESSON: Page 44 Twelve-year old Johnny Turnbull (aka "JT") has spent his entire life in deep space... until his parents, and the parents of 200 other kids, decide to emigrate to the Rings of Orbis, a galactic trading center built around a black hole. During the transport, disaster strikes the ship, killing all the adults. When the children arrive at the Rings, they are forced to become indentured servants who must work off the debt their parents incurred to make the trip. Just as JT can communicate directly with their ship's computer, he can also interface with the giant, all-knowing, all-

Questions to Ask When Choosing Books

When browsing the bookstore or library for books to use when teaching about organization, ask yourself:

- Does the author give me something interesting to think about right from the start? Do I want to keep reading?

- In the body of the book, does the author use a variety of sequence words, such as *later, then,* and *meanwhile,* and transition words, such as *however, because, also,* and *for instance*? Does he or she clearly connect ideas from sentence to sentence and from paragraph to paragraph?

- Is it easy to follow the author's points? Are the details well placed? Does the organization support the book's main idea?

- Is the ending satisfying? Has the author wrapped up all the loose ends and left me with something to think about?

controlling computer that operates the Rings. He is, in fact, "a softwire," an evolutionary anomaly who can enter and control all electronic devices. This story is great fun, largely because of the detailed descriptions of the residents of the Rings. At its heart is a story of immigration. Haarsma wastes no time in establishing the story's basic premise, which is that life as an immigrant often means being looked down upon, feared, and misunderstood.

Instead of Three Wishes
Megan Whalen Turner
HarperCollins, 1995

The seven short stories here, each with a touch of magic, revolve around solving unusual problems. In the title story, "Instead of Three Wishes," an eccentric elf insists he repay a favor to a young woman who doesn't want to be repaid. In "The Nightmare," a bully gets what he deserves. In "The Baker King," an identity switch doesn't have the expected result. In "Aunt Charlotte and the NGA Portraits," a magical painting holds treasure for an adventurous girl. In "A Plague of Leprechauns," leprechaun seekers far outnumber the leprechauns themselves. In "The Factory," one job provides spectral views of the past. "Leroy Roachbane" follows a young man from modern times to medieval Sweden where he successfully applies his knowledge of pest control. Each story is tightly organized, transitions neatly into its conflict, and has a satisfying conclusion. Turner is adept at quickly establishing each story's conflict and moving on to its resolution.

Key Quality: Using Sequence Words and Transition Words

Beautiful Warrior: The Legend of the Nun's Kung Fu
Emily Arnold McCully, author and illustrator
Scholastic, 1998

Sequence words, such as *initially* and *finally*, and transition words, such as *instead* and *meanwhile*, are not the most glamorous elements of writing, but they're essential. Every story writer uses them as touch points to move the narrative along. But few use them as well as Emily Arnold McCully does in *Beautiful Warrior*. In fact, she uses them so well, the reader barely notices them. As a result, her story flows like a ribbon of fine silk. In it, young Jingyong has no interest in pursuing idle pastimes girls typically pursue in China's ancient Forbidden City. Instead, she chooses kung fu. Jingyong grows up to become a Buddhist nun committed to the five pillars of learning: art, literature, music, medicine, and, most especially, martial arts. In time, she meets Mingyi, a peasant girl, and teaches her the physical and spiritual skills she needs to escape an abusive arranged marriage. A powerful story of two powerful women.

The Journey: Stories of Migration

Cynthia Rylant
Lambert Davis, illustrator
Scholastic, 2006

It's impossible for a writer to describe the concept of migration without using transition words and sequence words because, let's face it, the concept itself is all about transitioning and sequencing—the transition of animals moving from one place to another, and the sequence of events that occur as they make that transition. In *The Journey: Stories of Migration*, Cynthia Rylant describes this phenomenon in her trademark poetic style. She examines six very different animals—locust, whale, eel, butterfly, caribou, and tern—that have one thing in common: a biological clock that tells them to travel for reasons of survival. The monarch butterfly escapes deadly cold. The gray whale seeks food. The caribou gives birth. These are amazing stories, filled with danger, delight, and wonder. Share them with students as bite-sized examples of well-organized writing.

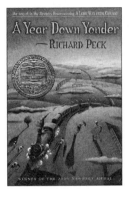

A Year Down Yonder

Richard Peck
Penguin, 2000

FOCUS LESSON: Page 46 When Mary Alice arrives at Grandma Dowdel's home in a small town in downstate Illinois, the future looks dim. The Great Depression has left her parents unable to afford life for themselves and two children in Chicago. So her brother has gone off to work in the Conservation Corps, while Mary Alice has been sent to live with Grandma until her parents can get back on their feet. At first, Grandma Dowdel doesn't seem kid-friendly. In fact, she's all business. But over time, she surprises Mary Alice—and teaches her some important lessons about being a lady, getting the best out of men, helping people in need, and taking pride in who she is and what she stands for. This sequel to *A Long Way from Chicago* is based on Peck's own adolescence, growing up in Decatur, Illinois, during the Depression. As such, he has a talent for capturing what is most uplifting and iconic about rural America. Peck leads the reader through the story with sequence and transition words that make the significance of each event clear.

The Westing Game

Ellen Raskin
Penguin, 1978

Who will solve the mystery presented in millionaire industrialist Sam Westing's will and receive $200,000,000? When 16 heirs are called to a reading of that will, they find themselves embroiled in a mystery composed of false leads, red herrings, reversed clues, and plenty of jokes played upon them. Each person is paired with another person and paid $10,000 just for participating. Each pair gets a set of clues made up of words from *America the Beautiful*, but exactly how to interpret the clues proves almost impossible. The story covers many years, and multiple smaller mysteries are solved along the way before anyone solves the big mystery: Who killed Sam? (That is, of course, if he really is dead.) Raskin has crafted an intricate mystery plot, carefully using sequence and transition words to make sure readers are in possession of just the right information to control the direction of their thinking.

My Father, the Angel of Death
Ray Villareal
Arte Público, 2006

The worst thing about being the son of a professional wrestling star may be that "friends" want to come to your home just to meet your dad. It may also be that people expect you to have all your father's ringside machismo, not realizing it's all an act. Mild-mannered Jesse Baron knows all about the realities of professional wrestling; his father is the infamous "Angel of Death." So far, Mr. Baron's nomadic career has not lent itself to a stable family life. So when he moves the family to San Antonio, he promises to stay put and put his personal life first. When bullies attempt to steal lunch money from the girl of Jesse's dreams, Jesse finds a little Angel of Death inside of himself. Surprises are important in Villareal's story, and he uses sequence and transition words to set up his delivery of those surprises with maximum impact.

Forged by Fire
Sharon M. Draper
Simon & Schuster, 1998

In this prequel to *Tears of a Tiger*, Sharon M. Draper steps into the earlier life of Gerald Nickleby. Before he became an aspiring basketball star in *Tears*, Gerald had already faced unbelievable challenges in life, including a stepfather who physically assaulted him and sexually assaulted his own daughter, the death of a friend, and a fiery brush with his own death. Needless to say, Gerald's life as a child and teen is horrendous, but it is also compelling and inspiring. Draper has a gift for telling the stories of young people who live lives that society in general seems to know little about. Winner of the 1997 United States Teacher of the Year Award and five-time winner of the Coretta Scott King Award, she knows about schools and kids and the lives they lead. Like most Draper novels, this one has a fast pace, and the author's transition and sequence words serve as crucial road signs to keep readers from careening off-track. (Mature Themes)

Key Quality: Structuring the Body

The Wall: Growing Up Behind the Iron Curtain

Peter Sís, author and illustrator
Farrar, Straus and Giroux, 2007

During the Cold War, the Eastern Bloc countries of Poland, Hungary, and Czechoslovakia, among others, were ideologically and physically separated from our Western world. The most conspicuous symbol of the war, of course, was Germany's Berlin Wall, a stretch of concrete and steel, dividing the capitalist West from the communist East. In this visually stunning memoir of his life in Czechoslovakia, Peter Sís brings life under communist rule to chilling reality—with its censorship, deprivation, and degradation. The book is an extended time line, beginning in 1948, with the Soviet takeover of Sís's homeland, and ending in 1991, with the breakup of the Soviet Union. Illustrations depict key events, while the running text at the bottom of each page explains what was happening in Sís's life during each of those events. As a result, the reader gets a very public and personal glimpse at a controversial episode in recent history.

Meanwhile Back at the Ranch

Trinka Hakes Noble
Tony Ross, illustrator
Dial Books, 1987

FOCUS LESSON: Page 47

In this crazy spin on American Gothic, Rancher Hicks decides to drive into Sleepy Gulch to see what's happening, while his wife Elna stays behind to dig potatoes. Who's in for a better time? Most readers would place their bet on Rancher Hicks. But it's Elna who winds up having all the fun—and making a fortune! While Rancher Hicks checks out 12-year-old wanted posters at the post office, Elna wins "a brand-new wall-to-wall frost-free super-cool refrigerator." While he gets the latest gossip at the barber shop, she receives a winning lottery ticket. While he eats potatoes (and only potatoes) at Millie's Mildew Luncheonette, she strikes oil in the potato field. While he watches a checker game at the general store, she's transformed into a movie star by a Hollywood producer. Noble presents the story in "real time" by alternating between ranch and town throughout the book. An organizational tour de force!

Crossing Jordan

Adrian Fogelin
Peachtree Publishers, 2000

When he hears that the Lewises, an African-American family, will be moving in next door, Cass Bodine's father says the "place is gonna go downhill" and builds a tall fence that "even Michael Jordan couldn't see over." Mr. Bodine is determined to keep the new family from mixing with his own. Regardless, Cass meets Jemmie Lewis through a knothole in the fence and challenges her to a footrace. The two seventh graders become inseparable friends, dubbing themselves "Chocolate Milk." Before the summer is over, Jemmie's mother, a nurse, saves the Bodine baby from near fatal exposure to the Florida heat, Cass and Jemmie finish a charity race for sickle-cell anemia and unite the community in the process, and Mr. Bodine's tolerance of his neighbors undergoes a 180-degree turnaround. Jemmie and Cass demonstrate the possibilities of friendship when we are free to befriend whomever we choose. The change of heart that some of Fogelin's characters experience unfolds powerfully in a series of cause-and-effect events.

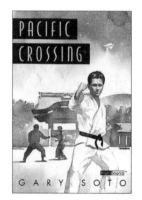

Pacific Crossing

Gary Soto
Harcourt, Inc., 1992

Lincoln Mendoza and his friend Tony take the wrong San Francisco bus and wind up in Japantown, where they discover a martial arts school and begin taking classes there. When they are offered a summer exchange trip to Japan, Lincoln imagines himself and Tony practicing kempo on tatami mats in a majestic dojo, under the guidance of a tough, young karate master. But much to his surprise, the dojo is nothing more than a lawn and his instructor is Mrs. Oyama, a fifty-seven-year-old woman. The cultural exchange goes both ways; one of the boys in Lincoln's host family, Mitsuo, is surprised to find that all Americans do not carry guns and has trouble understanding how Lincoln could possibly be both Mexican and American. At summer's end, Lincoln returns to San Francisco with insights very different from the ones he was expecting before he left. His complete turnabout is believable largely because of Soto's careful construction of the body of the novel.

American Born Chinese

Gene Yang
First Second/Roaring Brook, 2006

Jin Wang has just moved to a new neighborhood and started at a new school. Like most of the kids there, he was born in the United States. His teacher and classmates, however, assume that he emigrated from Asia and immediately impose stereotypes on him: he surely eats dogs and he is here to wed the only other Asian American in their class, in an arranged marriage. Along with the realistic story of Jin

Wang, Gene Yang gives us two parallel fantasy stories, one about the Monkey King, a parody of traditional Chinese legend, and the other about Danny and Chin-Kee, the tale of two cousins, one who rejects Chinese culture and one who embraces it with all his heart. The three stories in this graphic novel culminate in a revealing ending that captures beautifully the book's overarching theme: the complexities of identity as imposed by self and others. The book's body is structured to move the three stories forward without giving away that they are always converging.

Downriver
Will Hobbs
Laurel Leaf, 1995

Climbing 13,000-foot mountains and rafting western whitewater rivers may be what Discovery Unlimited is all about on the surface, but what it's really about is helping troubled youths find their better selves. And it's working. The participating teenagers, who refer to themselves as "Hoods in the Woods," have not elected to (literally) blow their whistles, the sign that they've had enough and want to go home. However, during a rafting expedition through the Grand Canyon under the supervision of Al, their wilderness guide/counselor, the kids revert to their old ways by stealing all the equipment and launching from a forbidden point in the river that starts out calm but leads to deadly hazards for the wayward youngsters. Told through the eyes of Jessie, a fifteen-year-old girl placed in Discovery Unlimited by her father, *Downriver* has the day-to-day feel of reality. Thoughtful structuring of the body pairs real hazards in the Grand Canyon with the emotional and psychological growth of the characters.

Key Quality: Ending With a Sense of Resolution

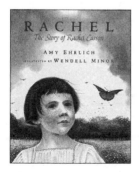

Rachel: The Story of Rachel Carson
Amy Ehrlich
Wendell Minor, illustrator
Harcourt, Inc., 2003

Rachel Carson's brilliant book, *Silent Spring*, is, in our eyes, the most significant plea ever written for environmental education. First published in 1962, it is often considered the spark that ignited today's green movement. With this picture-book biography, children learn about Carson and her important work. It is filled with beautiful, passionate language, right to the final paragraph: ". . . just as the butterflies had their own cycle of life, so did each human being. Her time was nearing its end, but the rhythms of nature would go on. Spring would follow winter. Fish still swam in the ocean and the birds were singing." Ehrlich offers a tribute to this pioneer of environmental writing and helps us appreciate her contributions in whole new ways.

No!
David McPhail, author and illustrator
Roaring Brook Press, 2009

Some of the best picture books are just that: *picture* books, with no words at all. Take David McPhail's *No!* for example, the simple story of a boy who sets out to mail a letter, and encounters a number of dangerous hurdles along the way—cannon fire, an air strike, a police raid, a dog attack, and, finally, a run-of-the-mill bully. However, by daring to utter one simple word—"No!"—the boy not only mails his letter, but transforms his town from a war zone into a place of peace and harmony. *No!* is a riveting book. With virtually no writing, though, how can it help middle schoolers become better writers? By prompting them to put language to pictures: McPhail's mesmerizing, magical illustrations draw students in and invite them to tell the story in their own words and, in the process, become better storytellers—and better storytellers become better writers.

Lily Quench and the Black Mountains
Natalie Jane Prior
Penguin, 2001

Lily Quench rides on the back of Queen Dragon, battling evil. The dragon's primary weapon is her fiery breath, while Lily's is "quenching drops," which are normally used against dragons, but also against tanks and any other form of martial machinery. Unfortunately, Lily's drops have run out just as the Black Count is hatching a plot to invade the peaceful kingdom of Ashby, where Lily and Queen Dragon reside. Lily and Queen Dragon must go into the forbidding Black Mountains in search of the blue lily, a crucial ingredient of quenching drops. Along the way, Queen Dragon faces her fears, Lily makes a new friend, and the Black Count escapes to cause mischief in future books. Prior borrows a little from Roald Dahl's *Matilda* to create a self-reliant and precocious young girl who has no fear of evil adults. Readers will have no problem recognizing the story's physical climax and the protagonist's emotional climax.

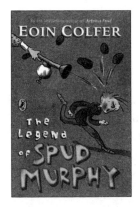

The Legend of Spud Murphy
Eoin Colfer
Hyperion, 2004

When the five Woodman brothers and their fifteen rowdy friends are more than the Woodman parents can stand, Mr. Woodman decides that Will and Marty "need something to do this summer: Something to get you out of the house," maybe even "something educational." Their parents decide that the library is the perfect place for the boys, where Mrs. Spud Murphy, head librarian, will supervise them. The boys are horrified: Mrs. Murphy was a spy in the army, used for "[t]racking down kids from enemy countries," and she is well known for taking down miscreants with her legendary potato shooter. Despite all that, Marty decides to test Mrs. Murphy on the first day by switching books out of their places, but she proves to be more than a match for him. Then one day, a miracle happens: Will becomes a reader. He finds and devours book after fascinating book. This book ends with the resolution of two conflicts: the battle of wills between Mrs. Murphy and the boys, and the boys' struggle to embrace reading.

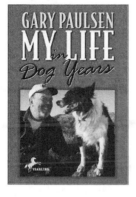

My Life in Dog Years

Gary Paulsen
Random House, 1998

In an effort to honor the dogs in his life, Paulsen writes what might be called a dog autobiography, a collection of stories about eight memorable dogs he's had the pleasure to know over the years. From Snowball, Paulsen's first dog, who saved him from a poisonous snake in the Philippines, to Josh, a border collie who is practically human, Paulsen pays tribute to each of his four-legged best friends. There's Quincy, the smallest but bravest, and Caesar, the largest but most timid. Paulsen saves one of the best stories for last and definitely one that leaves the reader on an emotional high. From career farm dogs to loyal Labradors to back-alley brawlers, Paulsen creates canine archetypes from life experience. This book will leave readers reminiscing happily about canines in their own past.

The Skin I'm In

Sharon G. Flake
Jump at the Sun, 1998

FOCUS LESSON: Page 49

Maleeka Madison has excellent grades and a talent for writing. Nevertheless, at her under-resourced urban school, she is an outcast because of her dark skin and her worn-out wardrobe. Even though Maleeka's time and energy is dominated by helping her mother, who suffers from depression, a new teacher, Miss Saunders, places additional expectations on her. Miss Saunders sees Maleeka's potential and encourages her to try her hand at creative writing. Encouraged by her newfound confidence, Maleeka faces her tormentors and unexpectedly touches a classmate's heart. Told from Maleeka's point of view, this story contains language that feels very real. As the story's multiple conflicts reach their peak, so does Maleeka's own personal growth.

Focus Lesson 1: Creating the Lead

CHAPTER BOOK

The Softwire: Virus on Orbis 1
PJ Haarsma

Think About the Writer's Work:

- Did he give the reader something interesting to think about right from the start?

- Will the reader want to keep reading?

- Has he tried to get the reader's attention?

- Did he let the reader know what is coming?

Lesson Focus:

Twelve-year-old Johnny Turnbull lives aboard the seed-ship *Renaissance* that is traveling to the Rings of Orbis. Before Johnny and the other young travelers were born, all the adults died; the orphans were stored as embryos and raised by the space ship's computer. When they finally arrive on Orbis 1, they are horrified to find they are expected to work as slaves for the Guarantors (alien businessmen). Johnny controls the computer with his mind and uses his gift to free himself and find out what really happened to the generation that came before. In this lesson, students examine Haarsma's action-packed introduction and the war in which he draws readers into the story from the first lines. They examine other books for leads and try writing their own.

Materials:

- a copy of *The Softwire: Virus on Orbis 1*

- projection and copies of the Think About the Writer's Work questions above

- paper, pens, pencils

- projection of the following passage from Chapter 1:

> "I can see them! I can see the Rings of Orbis!" Theodore Malone cried, and a stampede of kids charged toward the observation deck.
>
> I bet you're dying to see Orbis, aren't you, malf?" Randall Switzer said, digging his foot a little deeper into my face. In fact, I was. I'd waited twelve years to see my new home, wishing every day was this day. But I wouldn't dare let him know that.
>
> "I can kill a little more time down here," I said from the floor.
>
> Switzer snickered and shifted more weight onto his foot. I hate feet. Feet with shoes, feet with socks, but worse of all—like the sweaty one grinding into my cheek—I hate bare feet.
>
> "What are you doing, Switzer?" Maxine Bennett said.
>
> "Why do you care?" he replied.
>
> "I figure you've got another microsecond before Mother knows what you're doing. I do not want to be near all this food when it turns the gravity off," Max warned him.
>
> *You don't want to be on a toilet, either,* I thought but I didn't feel this was the right time to bring that up.

What to Do:

1. Share with students the Think About the Writer's Work questions and discuss the importance of creating strong leads in writing. Ask students to share some of their favorite techniques for beginning a piece. They might suggest a quotation, a question, an introduction of a character, entering into the middle of the action of the story, a definition of a key term that readers don't know and will be important to the story, and so on.

2. Ask students to find three types of text and examine each one's lead. Make a T-chart. Label column #1 "text type" and column #2 "technique." Then, as a class, fill in the chart.

3. Tell students you are going to read the introduction to a science fiction novel called *The Softwire: Virus on Orbis 1* by PJ Haarsma. Project the passage from page 44, read it aloud, and have students listen carefully and follow along. When you've finished reading, ask whether Haarsma's lead engages them enough to make them want to hear you read more.

4. Ask students to name the technique Haarsma used to begin his novel—using dialogue between characters who are already engaged in the action of the story. Compare that technique to others students found and add it to the list if it isn't there already.

5. Put students in groups of three or four. Ask them to look at the projected lead and name everything Haarsma was able to accomplish in it:

   - Introduce two main characters

   - Create a good guy and a bad guy

   - Establish a character's personality

   - Provide a setting and time (in the future)

   - Give details about plot content

6. Ask students to read the lead of a book that everyone in the class knows, such as *Charlotte's Web*, *Where the Red Fern Grows*, or *Harry Potter and the Sorcerer's Stone*, and have them write a new lead that conveys as much information as the original and answers the Think About the Writer's Work questions.

7. Share the leads students write. Discuss which are the most engaging and why.

Lesson Extension:

Have students make lists of lead types and put them in their writer's notebooks or wherever they keep writing tips for reference as they write. Ask them to indicate which leads might work best for fiction and which for nonfiction, and code each lead type appropriately.

Focus Lesson 2: Using Sequence Words and Transition Words

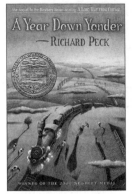

YOUNG ADULT NOVEL

A Year Down Yonder
Richard Peck

Think About the Writer's Work:

- Has he used sequence words such as *later, then*, and *meanwhile*?
- Did he use a variety of transition words such as *however, because, also,* and *for instance*?
- Has he shown how ideas connect from sentence to sentence?
- Does his organization make sense from paragraph to paragraph?

Lesson Focus:

It's 1937, the height of the Great Depression, and fifteen-year-old Mary Alice is sent from Chicago to the country to live with her grandmother, whom she hardly knows. At first, she's less than enthusiastic about living in a place that's as strange to her as her grandmother. But she learns to appreciate life there and even comes to regret leaving once her parents are back on their feet. Students examine a passage from this finely written book which contains sequence words and transition words, then write a continuation of the passage, using sequence words and transition words.

Materials:

- a copy of *A Year Down Yonder*
- projection and copies of the Think About the Writer's Work questions above
- paper, pens, pencils
- projection of the following passage from the chapter entitled "Away in a Manger":

> "After I'd dried the dishes, I opened up my homework. They had homework down here, too, sadly. Miss Butler could really dole it out. Mr. Herkimer was no slouch. Grandma sat at the other end of the table, nodding, while I tried to diagram some sentences.
> I moved on to biology, falling into the rhythm of Grandma's snore. A Seth Thomas steeple clock stood on a high shelf. When it struck ten, Grandma jerked awake. She looked around the room astonished. It was her belief that she never slept, not even in bed."

What to Do:

1. Show the Think About the Writer's Work questions and discuss. Ask students to look around the room and see if they spot sequence words or transition words on the walls, doors, bulletin boards, and so forth. On the board, list any they find.

2. Ask students to get into pairs, select a book from the classroom library, open it to any page, read it together, and call out or jot down any sequence words or transition words

Organization

they find. Ask them how the writers showed the logical sequence of ideas if he or she did not use specific sequence words or transition words.

3. Make a detailed class list of ways authors show sequence and create transitions. The list may include key sequence words, such as *next* and *later*, or transition words and phrases, such as *furthermore* and *all in all*. The list might also include context clues such as identifying the antecedent before using a pronoun or the use of verb tense to show passage of time. If time allows, invite students to locate a list of commonly used sequence and transition words and phrases on the Internet.

4. Summarize the plot of *A Year Down Yonder* and discuss how it might feel to leave your home and live with a relative you hardly know.

5. Project the passage above and read it aloud. Ask students to call out any sequence and transition words they spot. Underline those words.

6. Ask students to think about other ways Peck connects ideas from sentence to sentence and paragraph to paragraph. They might notice, for instance, that he wrote the entire passage in past tense, which explains to the reader when the events took place in a logical time frame.

7. Brainstorm with students what might happen next. After Mary Alice completes her homework and Grandmother wakes up from her quick nap, perhaps Mary Alice talks to Grandmother or plays a game with her before going to bed. Or perhaps Grandmother tells Mary Alice a story from her youth.

8. Ask student pairs to extend the story by at least one paragraph. Tell them to be sure to use several sequence words and transition words to show order. They should keep the tense in mind as they write, too.

9. When they've finished, have students share their pieces, noting each sequence and transition word as it is read.

Lesson Extension:

Read aloud the next page of the book, to the section break. Discuss how Peck links ideas using sequence and transition words and uses other organizational strategies students notice.

Focus Lesson 3: Structuring the Body

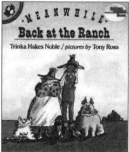

PICTURE BOOK

Meanwhile Back at the Ranch
Trinka Hakes Noble

Think About the Writer's Work:

- Has she shown the reader where to slow down and where to speed up?

- Do all the details fit where they are placed?

- Will the reader find it easy to follow her ideas?

- Does the book's organization help the main idea stand out?

Lesson Focus:

Rancher Hicks heads into town to find some excitement, leaving his wife, Elna, back at the ranch. However, as Noble gradually and cleverly reveals, it's Elna who has all the fun, while her husband gets a shave, plays checkers, watches a turtle cross the road, and engages in other equally mundane activities. In this lesson, students use the comparison/contrast structure of this delightful book to create "Meanwhile Back at School" stories.

Materials:

- a copy of *Meanwhile Back at the Ranch*
- projection and copies of the Think About the Writer's Work questions above
- projections of selected illustrations and passages
- paper, pens, pencils

What to Do:

1. Project the Think About the Writer's Work questions, discuss them with students, and list different structures for organizing the body of text such as chronological events, comparison/contrast, cause and effect, point-by-point analysis, problem and solution, deductive logic, and order of importance.

2. Tell students you are going to read a hilarious story to them. As they listen, be sure they consider how Noble organizes the body of the text so it flows logically.

3. Read *Meanwhile Back at the Ranch*, using a document camera to project the pages or simply showing pictures as you go. When you finish, ask students to tell you the structure Noble used to organize the writing. They may mention several, including chronological events and comparison/contrast.

4. Ask them to check the Think About the Writer's Work questions and pick the dominant structure: comparison/contrast. Note that Noble repeats a transition word, "Meanwhile…" to signal a change in setting.

5. Tell students they are going to write their own versions of the story using the comparison/contrast structure. Their stories will be called, "Meanwhile Back at [name of your school]".

6. Ask the class to call out different things a middle school student might look forward to doing if he or she were to stay home from school for a day: watch TV, play video games, eat lots of junk food, sleep, and so on. Then ask them what might keep these things from actually happening: a power outage, no groceries, an annoying little brother or sister, a beeping smoke detector with a low battery, and so on.

7. Ask students to generate a list of exciting things that might happen at school: a visit from a professional sports team, free pizza and ice cream, thousand-dollar bills given out by the principal, unlimited lunch and/or recess time, chauffeured trips to the shopping mall, and so on.

8. Put students into groups of three or four and give one group the job of deciding the identity of the two main characters, naming them, and telling why one stayed home while the other went to school. Give another group the job of ending the story—the wrap-up. Divide the remaining groups into two sections: One section will take on

the role of a student who stays home from school expecting to have a great day, but is sorely disappointed; the other section will take the role of a student at school enjoying an unexpectedly wonderful day. Ask students to write out what happens, using the transition word *meanwhile*, as Noble does in her book.

9. When everyone finishes writing, ask groups to read their piece, beginning with the group who creates the main characters and sets up the story, then alternating between what happens at home and school, and finally ending with the group that wraps up the story.

10. Discuss how having a clear organizational structure, such as comparison/contrast, helps the ideas stand out and makes the writing easier to follow.

Lesson Extension:

Invite students to continue working on the story by smoothing out the flow of ideas and creating a picture book entitled "Meanwhile, Back at [name of your school]."

Focus Lesson 4: Ending With a Sense of Resolution

YOUNG ADULT NOVEL

The Skin I'm In
Sharon G. Flake

Think About the Writer's Work:

- Has she wrapped up all the loose ends?
- Did she end at the best place?
- Did she use an ending that makes the writing feel finished?
- Did she leave the reader with something to think about?

Lesson Focus:

Maleeka is used to being teased at school—about her clothes and her excellent grades, but mostly about her dark skin. Though she's good-natured and tries to ignore what others say, the taunts hurt and make her feel insecure. One day, a tough new seventh-grade teacher shows up, Miss Saunders, who has skin problems that are hard to ignore. Meleeka learns from Miss Saunders how to develop a completely different attitude about being different. In this lesson, students consider possible endings for this powerful book and then compare their ideas to Flake's actual ending.

Materials:

- a copy of *The Skin I'm In*
- projection of the Think About the Writer's Work questions above
- Types of Endings reproducible, page 51

- paper, pens, pencils
- projection of the book's ending from Chapter 32:

> When I finally walk into class, everybody's staring at me like I got two heads. I'm late, but Miss Saunders doesn't make an issue of it today.
>
> Class is in the detention room, while Miss Saunders's room is being repaired. Miss Saunders is giving us twenty pages of Ali Baba and the Forty Thieves to read by tomorrow and telling us she's been easy on us so far, but things are about to heat up.
>
> "Welcome back, Miss Madison," Miss Saunders says, giving me a wink. "Class wouldn't be the same unless you were late."
>
> Everybody laughs and turns my way. "Yeah," John-John says, "welcome back."

What to Do:

1. Summarize the plot of *The Skin I'm In*. Make sure students understand several key issues: (1) the main character, seventh grader Maleeka Madison, is smart and talented. She writes stories as a creative outlet because she is often treated badly by her peers, is sad about the loss of her father, and feels uncomfortable about how dark her skin is. (2) Maleeka goes to extremes to get her peers to like her, but no matter what she does, they still pick on her. (3) The new teacher, Miss Saunders, is tough, really tough, and has white blotches on her body, caused by a skin disorder.

2. Show the Think About the Writer's Work questions, hand out the Types of Endings reproducible, and discuss both with the class. *Do not* tell students Flake's ending, though.

3. Ask students to choose one of the types of endings and come up with an ending that is a natural extension of the summary you have provided. For example:

   The students stop teasing Maleeka and start harassing Miss Saunders. Maleeka joins in, even though she knows it's wrong. All the students are put into detention by the principal, realize the error of their ways, and apologize to the new teacher. (Moral)

   Maleeka gets tired of being tormented and decides to transfer to a new school, but nothing changes. Her classmates are just as cruel there. (Irony)

   Maleeka writes a revealing story about the kids who have treated her badly and makes them realize how wrong they've been. She becomes good friends with all of them. (Epiphany)

4. Project and read Flake's ending, which is a "Hollywood Ending." Talk about how she ties up the story's loose ends and concludes on a high note.

5. Discuss the importance of providing readers with strong endings and encourage students to revise the ending to a piece they are working on.

Lesson Extension:

Invite each student to bring in three fiction books and three nonfiction books from the library, compare the endings, and discuss any differences they notice. Can students name the type of ending the author used in each book, using the reproducible and/or coming up with their own ideas?

Types of Endings

Epiphany wraps up the story with a sudden insight by the character

Moral reveals a lesson for the reader

Image provides a visual connection to a key point in the story

Irony notes the incongruity between what the character says and does and how the story turns out

Tragedy ends on a dark note, prompting the reader to consider how the final events reveal the theme

Surprise ends with an unexpected turn of events

Hollywood Ending provides the perfect ending, in which everything works out fine

From "How to Write a Strong Ending in Fiction" by C. Scott (2008), adapted for middle school.

Focus Lesson

CHAPTER 3

Voice

❝Good writing teaches the learning writer about style, graceful narration, plot development, the creation of believable characters, and truth-telling. . . . You cannot hope to sweep someone else away by the force of your writing until it has been done to you.**❞**

—STEPHEN KING from *On Writing: A Memoir of the Craft*

Has anyone ever recommended a book to you by saying something like, "You just have to read this book. It's so ordinary and predictable. After just two pages, you will be so bored you'll never remember a thing. Seriously, it's impossible to pick it up." No? That has never happened to us either.

Avid readers are more likely to say just the opposite. They yearn to find a fellow-reader who will pick up a best-loved book and, when he or she is finished reading it, talk about it in luxurious detail. And one of the things that makes an avid reader recommend a book in the first place is voice. It's voice that keeps us reading, after all—that seemingly magical connection between the writer and the reader. If you start Sherman Alexie's *Absolutely True Diary of a Part-Time Indian,* you will not be the same person when you finish it. If you don't shed a tear as you read Patricia Polocco's *Pink and Say,* you didn't really read it. And if you don't feel the struggle between culture and self-identity while reading *Beneath My Mother's Feet* by Amjed Qamar, you must find it hard to understand why everyone doesn't think and feel just like you do. These books have the power to bowl over and transform readers by the sheer force of the writer's voice. They will sweep you away.

Voice is the tone and tenor of the piece—the personal stamp of the writer, which is achieved through a strong understanding of purpose and audience. It's the force behind the words that proves a real person is speaking and cares about what is being said. Writers engage the reader with voice, drawing him or her in by making connections between the reader's life and the piece's topic. They have a solid handle on why and for whom they're writing the piece, and choose an appropriate voice—cheerful or melancholy, humorous or serious, confident or uncertain, confrontational or conciliatory, fanciful or authoritative, and so on.

Voice is the heart and soul of the writing—its very life. When writers are dedicated to the topic, they apply voice almost automatically because they are passionate about what they are saying and how they are saying it. They inject a flavor that is unmistakably their own and that distinguishes them from all other writers. To create strong voice, the writer must apply with skill and confidence the following key qualities:

✳ **Establishing a Tone**
  The writer cares about the topic, and it shows. The writing is expressive and compelling. The reader feels the writer's conviction, authority, and integrity.

✳ **Conveying the Purpose**
  The writer makes clear his or her reason for creating the piece. He or she offers a point of view that is appropriate for the mode (narrative, expository, or persuasive), which compels the reader to read on.

✳ **Creating a Connection to the Audience**
  The writer speaks in a way that makes the reader want to listen. He or she has considered what the reader needs to know and the best way to convey it by sharing his or her fascination, feelings, and opinions about the topic.

✳ **Taking Risks to Create Voice**
  The writer expresses ideas in new ways, which makes the piece interesting and original. The writing sounds like the writer because of his or her use of distinctive, just-right words and phrases.

Voice has the power to create itself. When all other traits are fully functioning, it emerges naturally. But that doesn't mean it's easy to create. It results from passion, conviction, integrity, and a clear understanding of purpose and audience.

Mentor Texts in This Chapter

Establishing a Tone

I Am the Dog, I Am the Cat, Hall

The Memory Coat, Woodruff

When You Reach Me, Stead

Gathering Blue, Lowry

Coraline, Gaiman

Beneath My Mother's Feet, Qamar

Conveying the Purpose

Pink and Say, Polacco

The Fabulous Feud of Gilbert & Sullivan, Winter

The Million Dollar Kick, Gutman

The Cow-Tail Switch and Other West African Stories, Courlander

The Absolutely True Diary of a Part-Time Indian, Alexie

The Bully, Langan

Creating a Connection to the Audience

You Wouldn't Want to Be on Apollo 13! A Mission You'd Rather Not Go On, Graham

The Black Snowman, Mendez

Sassy: Little Sister Is Not My Name, Draper

Perloo the Bold, Avi

Rules, Lord

Jim Thorpe, Original All-American, Bruchac

Taking Risks to Create Voice

This Is Your Life Cycle, Miller

John, Paul, George & Ben, Smith

I Was a Sixth Grade Alien, Coville

The Transmogrification of Roscoe Wizzle, Elliott

What I Saw and How I Lied, Blundell

Hoot, Hiassen

Key Quality: Establishing a Tone

I Am the Dog, I Am the Cat

Donald Hall
Barry Moser, illustrator
Dial Books, 1994

FOCUS LESSON: Page 64 Famed poet Donald Hall presents alternating points of view of a tabby cat and a Rottweiler in this delightful book. Both pets report what they do in the course of a day. When it comes to eating, the dog enjoys bones. And he most definitely likes to be fed. The cat, on the other hand, doesn't care whether somebody's fed her or not, as long as she's eaten. The dog sleeps all night, while the cat stays awake to hunt mice... or rubber bands, paper clips, or pieces of paper. But what truly sets them apart is not what they say, but *how* they say it. The dog's tone, in Hall's words, is dignified, guilty, sprightly, obedient, friendly, vigilant, and soulful, for it is a dog, while the cat's is independent, selfish, fearless, beautiful, cuddly, scratchy, and intelligent, for it is a cat. Readers are sure to hear the uniquely feline and canine tones that Hall establishes for each animal.

The Memory Coat

Elvira Woodruff
Michael Dooling, illustrator
Scholastic, 1999

Life is good for Rachel, living in her Russian shtetl with her lively, loving extended family. That is until a tide of anti-Jewish sentiment sweeps the country, and it becomes frightfully clear that remaining there is far too dangerous. The family decides to emigrate to America, with only a few belongings and a lot of hope. At the Ellis Island immigration station, the family members need to make a good impression if they are to be accepted. This fact becomes all too real when an inspector marks Rachel's young cousin Grisha for deportation because of a minor eye injury and a tattered coat that his deceased mother gave him. But thanks to Rachel's quick thinking, Grisha is permitted to enter and begin a new life. Woodruff is a master storyteller. Rachel's story is her own and, at the same time, every immigrant's. It's a story of memory, faith, and the eternal power of love.

Voice

When You Reach Me

Rebecca Stead
Wendy Lamb Books, 2009

As twelve-year-old Miranda helps her mother prepare for an appearance as a contestant on the *$20,000 Pyramid*, life grows stranger every day. First of all, she loses her best friend, Sal, who abandons her after being attacked by Marcus, the new kid. Strangely enough, Marcus doesn't seem like a bad person, but this is not the only paradox in Miranda's life. She is getting notes from someone who obviously knows her, notes that refer to events in the future as if they've already happened. The notes warn her of impending trouble, but also suggest ways to prevent it. Her favorite book, *A Wrinkle in Time*, and the idea of time travel influence Miranda's perspectives. Set in 1979 in New York City, Stead's story is told in the voice of a typical adolescent who is sometimes confident, sometimes vulnerable, sometimes confused, and often in love with the possibilities of life. Although life-and-death incidents occur as the story evolves, Miranda's innocent and hopeful tone remains constant.

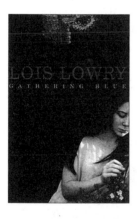

Gathering Blue

Lois Lowry
Delacorte, 2000

In this quasi-sequel to *The Giver*, Lowry again creates a dystopian future. A great apocalypse has left human survivors in low-tech villages with unchallenged social traditions. These traditions subjugate the needs of individuals to the needs of the larger group, establishing a climate of fear from the novel's beginning.

Each person is only as valuable as the contribution he or she can make to the village. When Kira's mother dies of "the sickness," Kira must face the Council of Guardians, which decides that she is still valuable even though a physical disability prevents her from performing manual labor. Kira has a greater skill. She can weave colored threads into a beautiful gown for the Singer, whose annual performance retells the story of civilization. As her new role in society unfolds, Kira comes to understand the ability of members of the Council to manipulate the path of civilization for good or evil. She comes to understand her own power, as well. As in *The Giver*, Lowry carefully maintains a neutral tone and lets events speak for themselves.

Questions to Ask When Choosing Books

When browsing the bookstore or library for books to use when teaching about voice, ask yourself:

- Can I name the book's primary voice (for example, fun-loving, irritated, knowledgeable, suspenseful, convincing)? Is the writing expressive? Does it sound as if the author cares about the topic?

- Is the purpose of the writing clear—to entertain, inform, explain, or maybe persuade? Does the author strike the right tone and have a clear point of view?

- Has the author thought about audience and, if so, has he or she captured the right voice for that audience? Will my students know how the author feels about the book's main topic?

- Is the writing interesting, fresh, and original? Has the author tried something different from what I've seen before in books for young people?

Coraline

Neil Gaiman
HarperCollins, 2002

When Coraline Jones's family moves into a large home sectioned off into flats, everything seems absolutely normal. That is, until Coraline discovers a sort of parallel universe within the building, specifically an apartment seemingly identical to her family's, inhabited by identical family members, with one exception: They have buttons for eyes. Her alternate mother, or "the Other Mother," is pleasant at first, but eventually shows her true colors. She turns out to be a wicked creature that recreates elements of the real world to trap children and imprison them in a mirror. When the Other Mother imprisons Coraline and then her family, a battle of wits ensues. Coraline needs to figure out the parameters of the Other Mother's alternate universe and find a way to rid the world of this demon forever. There is no better word to describe the tone of this book than *spooky*. Gaiman mixes the real with the surreal to make the story feel like the reader's own nightmare.

Beneath My Mother's Feet

Amjed Qamar
Atheneum, 2008

When Nazia's father is injured on a construction site in Karachi, Pakistan, and her brother runs away, her life changes. Nazia's mother finds work for the two of them cleaning the houses of wealthy residents of Karachi. Nazia drops out of school to devote time to earning money for her forthcoming wedding and her *jahez* (dowry). But circumstances worsen, and mother and daughter are left with no home, no jahez, and, at least for the time being, no marriage.

What Nazia gains, however, is an understanding of the importance of autonomy. As the men in the family desert the women and leave them to fend for themselves and their children, Nazia develops a new respect for her mother and all women. By the time the wedding is back on, Nazia refuses to let others control her destiny. Qamar portrays women as strong and capable, even in a society that treats them as second-class citizens. Qamar's resolute tone makes the reader feel as if Nazia and her mother's spirits will never be broken, no matter what atrocity is perpetrated on them.

Key Quality: Conveying the Purpose

Pink and Say

Patricia Polacco, author and illustrator
Philomel Books, 1994

In this heart-wrenching book, Patricia Polacco documents in words and pictures a Civil War story that has been passed down in her family for five generations. Sheldon Curtis, a 15-year-old Union soldier, is badly wounded in the field and left for dead. Things look bleak until he is saved by fellow Union soldier, Pinkus Aylee. Although the two boys are fighting for the same flag, there's something distinctly dissimilar about them: Sheldon is white and Pinkus is black. Pinkus carries Aylee to his home, where his kindhearted mother, Moe Moe Bay, nurses him back to health. However, they are ultimately captured and separated by Confederate soldiers, and only one of them survives. Polacco's purpose in writing the book—to keep Pink and Sheldon's story alive—couldn't be clearer, and she does it masterfully.

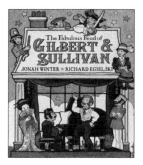

The Fabulous Feud of Gilbert & Sullivan

Jonah Winter
Richard Egielski, illustrator
Scholastic, 2009

Few creative collaborators are more legendary than William Schwenck Gilbert and Sir Arthur Sullivan. Chances are you've seen a production of at least one of their comic operas—perhaps *H.M.S. Pinafore, The Pirates of Penzance,* or *The Mikado.* But did you know that when these productions were first staged in the late 1800s the things happening behind the curtain were as dramatic as those happening on the stage? Gilbert and Sullivan fought like cats and dogs. The crux of their argument? Whether to continue creating publicly appealing work or start creating artistically groundbreaking work. In this exquisite example of narrative nonfiction, Jonah Winter gives us a glimpse inside the creative process of these men—with all its tension, suspense, and ultimate joy. Share it with your students to let them know that creating great work is never easy, but always rewarding.

The Million Dollar Kick

Dan Gutman
Hyperion, 2001

Whisper Nelson has a deep-seated psychological fear of soccer, probably because she scored a goal for the opposing team in her very first, and very last, game. She's the tallest girl in her class, doesn't run well, and lacks depth perception because of a vision problem. As such, she hates sports. So much so, she writes a paper about it for English class, "Why Sports Are a Waste." Whisper's little sister, Briana, on the other hand, is a phenomenon at soccer, basketball, and even boys' baseball. Fate often works in ironic ways, however. When Briana enters a contest to write a slogan for the local professional soccer team, the Oklahoma Kicks, Whisper signs the registration form because Briana is not old enough to do it herself. When Briana's entry, "The Kick Kick Butt," wins, Whisper has the chance to win the grand prize—one million dollars. But to succeed, she must go head-to-head with the Kick's goalie. Can Whisper score one (just one) kick against him? Gutman has created an entertaining and engaging story, in which the underdog is overwhelmed at times, but never defeated.

The Cow-Tail Switch and Other West African Stories

Harold Courlander and George Herzog
Madye Lee Chastain, illustrator
Henry Holt, 1947

As the introductory chapter of this collection of short stories points out, West Africa has changed in many ways over the centuries, "but many old things have not changed." And although many of the people of West Africa have moved, "they took their stories with them." Some of the 17 stories gathered in this collection have directly stated morals, like the title story, "The Cow-Tail Switch," which ends with "a man is not really dead until he is forgotten," and the story of the lazy rabbit and the industrious Guinea Fowl, which ends "The shortest path often goes nowhere." Others, such as "Kassa, the Strong One," require more probing, but are equally powerful. West African stories, some of which have inspired American folk tales such as "Br'er Rabbit," are fonts of cultural wisdom. Your students might enjoy comparing them to new and ancient stories from other cultures.

The Absolutely True Diary of a Part-Time Indian

Sherman Alexie
Little, Brown, 2007

FOCUS LESSON: Page 66 This National Book Award winner is one step removed from being pure autobiography. Alexie's protagonist, Arnold Spirit (aka Junior), experiences the same horrific medical maladies that Alexie himself did as a child; he is hydrocephalic, suffers from terrible vision, experiences seizures, and has ten-too-many teeth.

Also, just as Alexie did, Junior chooses not to attend Wellpinit High School with his friends and relatives on the Spokane Reservation, but instead attends the all-white Reardan High School, just off the reservation. Junior excels at basketball and academics, which makes him a hero at Reardan. But his friends on the reservation, who regard him as a traitor, alienate him. Alexie often uses humor to talk about the most painful parts of Junior's experience. His voice helps the reader process and understand the difficulties Junior faces, difficulties that might otherwise be too easy to deny. (Mature Themes)

The Bully
Paul Langan
Townsend Press, 2002

In this fifth offering from the Bluford series, Darrell Mercer moves from Philadelphia to southern California, where his small size puts him at the mercy of the local bullies. Back in Philadelphia, Darrell's size didn't matter to the young men from his neighborhood. But at Bluford High School it's all that matters. Darrell is on his own, until he joins the wrestling team and earns the respect of a new group of friends, friends who support him when he stands up to the bully who has been making his life miserable. This novel's voice is as defiant as Darrell, who refuses to accept anything less than victory and is willing to take his lumps to earn it. The Bluford's series' urban setting and African-American and Latino characters make for relevant reading for young people who may find life in affluent, white suburbs alienating. (Mature Themes)

Key Quality: Creating a Connection to the Audience

You Wouldn't Want to Be on Apollo 13! A Mission You'd Rather Not Go On
Ian Graham
David Antram, illustrator

World history is filled with the kinds of terrifying events most middle schoolers adore: wars, famines, plagues, natural and technological disasters... you name it. No group of books captures those events with more voice than those in the You Wouldn't Want to... series, which put readers in the heart of the action, regardless of how perilous it may be. With this book, they join the near-fatal Apollo 13 moon mission of April 1970. Graham tells kids everything—how the astronauts prepared for the mission, how they maneuvered the craft through outer space, and even how they went to the bathroom. But his focus, of course, is on how those astronauts survived a crippling explosion 204,431 miles from earth and found their way home—and he tells that story using a brilliant blend of suspense and humor. Clearly, Graham knows his audience and how to connect to it!

The Black Snowman

Phil Mendez
Carole Byard, illustrator
Scholastic, 1989

Being African American makes Jacob anything but proud. Mostly, it makes him bitter and angry. He resents that fact that he, his mother, and his younger brother, Peewee, live in poverty—and that "black" is a dirty word in history, literature, and everyday language. Things begin to change, though, when the two brothers build a snowman from the city's dirty snow. To their astonishment, the snowman comes to life when they place an African storyteller's kente cloth around its shoulders. The snowman tells Jacob about his rich cultural heritage—about the "strong, brave Africans from whom he descends." Jacob refuses to place himself in such prestigious company until Peewee's life is threatened and he is forced to use all the strength and bravery he can muster. In the process, Jacob discovers the magnificence in himself and his community.

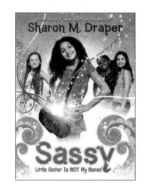

Sassy: Little Sister Is Not My Name

Sharon M. Draper
Scholastic, 2009

Sassy Simone Sanford is tired of being called "little sister," not just by her older brother and sister, but by her parents, too. She feels "pretty invisible" at home where she always gets the last of everything: last piece of chicken (a wing), last slice of bread (the heel), and last jelly bean in the bowl (licorice flavored). Sassy is very visible at school, however; she has lots of friends and a "Grammy" who is famous for dispensing stories and sharing wisdom around the world. When the city experiences a blackout, Sassy and her family are stuck in an elevator on the twenty-second floor of her mother's office building. Can someone as "invisible" as Sassy save her family? Sharon M. Draper connects to her audience by telling the story from Sassy's point of view and capturing just how it feels to be the youngest in the family.

Perloo the Bold

Avi
Scholastic, 1998

As someone who would much prefer reading about adventures to actually having them, Perloo is an unlikely hero. In fact, he wants nothing more than "a quiet simple life of reading and thinking." But when Jolaine the Good, wise and beloved leader of the rabbit-like Montmer tribe, proclaims Perloo her successor on her deathbed, he must find the courage to combat rivals and enemies alike. Using whatever resources he can summon, he defends his right to the throne against conniving Montmers and wins the respect of the coyote-like Felbarts, age-old enemies of the tribe. Along the way, he wins readers' respect as well, and their admiration and affection, too. The message here: Sometimes one must fight to create peace.

Rules

Cynthia Lord
Scholastic, 2006

FOCUS LESSON: Page 68 This is the story of twelve-year-old Catherine, who establishes rules for her autistic brother, David, in an attempt to help both of them cope with life. And the book is full of rules. In fact, each chapter heading conveys one. However, the rules seem to be more for Catherine's benefit than for David's. Some rules are very practical, such as "Don't stand in front of the TV when other people are watching it," while others are more philosophical, such as "Not everything worth keeping has to be useful," which ostensibly applies to antiques, but may have more to do with people. At the clinic where David has occupational therapy each week, Catherine meets some pretty interesting people, such as Jason, a paraplegic who uses word cards to communicate. Catherine has issues about what it means to be normal, issues that challenge her every day. But her heart is good and her imagination is boundless, and she will find her way. Readers will connect with her anxiety over individual differences among people and revel in her discovery that those differences should be celebrated.

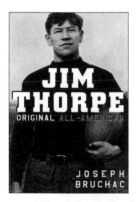

Jim Thorpe, Original All-American

Joseph Bruchac
Penguin, 2006

On July 15, 1912, Sweden's King Gustav V proclaimed to Native American sports legend James Frances Thorpe, "Sir, you are possibly the greatest athlete in the world." Indeed, Jim Thorpe is widely regarded as possibly the best athlete the world has ever seen. Winner of the pentathlon and decathlon in the 1912 Olympics, he was a physical and intellectual master of every sport he ever played, setting multiple records in his career, some of which still stand. In this fascinating biography of the Native American legend, Joseph Bruchac, author of over 60 young adult and children's books, tells Jim Thorpe's story in a voice that is at once friendly and determined, even in the face of terrible discrimination. Jim Thorpe's remarkable life is accurately recounted, thanks to Bruchac's conscientious research and a tone that reflects Thorpe's legendarily positive and hopeful personality.

Key Quality: Taking Risks to Create Voice

This Is Your Life Cycle

Heather Lynn Miller
Michael Chesworth, illustrator
Clarion Books, 2008

FOCUS LESSON: Page 70 Who says studying the life cycle of an insect has to be dull? When all the facts about it are folded into a game show–style narrative, as they are here, the result is not only interesting, but uproariously funny. In a crazy collection of text features such as diagrams, signs, speech bubbles, and voice-overs from host Bob Beetle, Miller honors "Dahlia the dragonfly," focusing on her birth and life in her pond habitat. Here's a taste from Dahlia's mother: "I found the perfect patch of swamp grass with tall, tender shoots. . . . I knew that laying my eggs inside would help keep you safe from hungry fish. By the end of the day, I had laid over 800 eggs. I was so exhausted when I finished, I just sat down and died." Bring this book into your classroom. Your students will be buzzing about it in no time. We guarantee it.

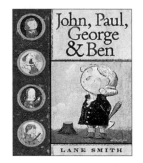

John, Paul, George & Ben

Lane Smith, author and illustrator
Hyperion, 2006

From the illustrator of the madcap *Stinky Cheese Man and Other Fairly Stupid Tales* comes this equally madcap bit of nonfiction that tells the tales of our founding fathers' formative years. John Hancock was a bold boy, Paul Revere was a noisy boy, George Washington was an honest boy, and Ben Franklin was a clever boy. And then there was Thomas Jefferson, who was fiercely independent . . . which is precisely why his name is not included in the title. The book is brimming with historical facts and hysterical language, packaged in a design that captures the colors, typography, and illustrations of Colonial times. It will appeal to students who aren't interested in American history by giving them a hilarious, human perspective on it, as well as to those who are interested in it by giving them information that, chances are, they don't already know.

I Was a Sixth Grade Alien

Bruce Coville
Simon & Schuster, 1999

With purple skin and a five-inch antenna on top of his head, Pleskit Meenom is definitely the weirdest sixth grader in Syracuse, New York. He came to be a member of Ms. Weintraub's class when his father, the first alien ambassador to Earth, insisted that his son attend public school. Pleskit worries about being accepted by his new peers on a planet where everyone likes "to pretend they're all unique and different, [but] at the same time each of them is desperately trying to be just like everyone else," and rightly so. When Jordan Lynch, the class bully, pushes Pleskit around, Pleskit blasts him into unconsciousness. The anti-alien forces seize the opportunity to mount a campaign to banish the new ambassador and his son from the planet, but classmate Tim Thompkins flies into action to help Pleskit prove that aliens are people, too. Told in alternating voices, chapter by chapter, this book is especially humorous when Pleskit tells his own story, complete with untranslatable alien words.

The Transmogrification of Roscoe Wizzle
David Elliott
Candlewick Press, 2001

Roscoe Wizzle lives in a pink house on Pleasant Street with his father, Waldo Wizzle, and his mother, Wilma Wizzle, who serves the family tuna surprise every other day because she "never got any kind of surprise at all" growing up in the city orphanage. Roscoe's life is pretty boring: "You get up in the morning and you look in the mirror and you think, *There I am. That's me, all right. And you don't think about it anymore.*" Life gets more exciting, however, when a new restaurant comes to town: Gussy's, home of Gussy the Gorilla and the Jungle Drum, a gigantic hamburger. Roscoe soon finds himself joyfully eating at Gussy's every day. But as the days go by, his friends notice something about him Roscoe himself doesn't notice: He is turning into a giant bug. With the help of the Institute for Science Gone Bad and a game of Monopoly, Roscoe solves the problem. Elliott takes a risk by expecting readers to identify with a teen-turned-insect, but makes it work beautifully.

What I Saw and How I Lied
Judy Blundell
Scholastic, 2008

In 1947, when her stepfather, Joe Spooner, takes fifteen-year-old Evie and her mother, Bev, to Palm Beach, Florida, on a sudden, unexpected vacation, it seems strange. They don't even take time to pack clothes or notify the school that Evie will be absent. Wearing a white bathing suit, like "a regular Rita Hayworth" appeals to Evie's gorgeous mom, though, so they take off. A number of new players enter their lives in Florida, including the Graysons, a wealthy couple who have a business proposal that could make the Spooners wealthy, and a handsome young veteran, Peter Coleridge, who claims to have been in Joe's unit in the war. Evie falls in love with Peter, who is not who he seems to be. When Peter dies at sea under suspicious conditions, and her stepfather is implicated, Evie finds that adulthood is not glamorous at all. Instead, it's filled with lies and scandal. This is a murder mystery wrapped in a classic coming-of-age story. The voice is part film noir and part Jane Austen. The late 1940s atmosphere is thick and enjoyable, and the suspense builds delectably as the story progresses. (Mature Themes)

Hoot
Carl Hiassen
Knopf, 2002

Roy Eberhardt has lived in ten different towns in almost as many years, so he is accustomed to the awkward transitions associated with starting over. Now a new student in Coconut Cove, Florida, he is more interested in the strange, shoeless boy he sees running through the yards, golf courses, and swamps than he is in his new classmates. Roy eventually befriends this strange boy, Napoleon Bridger Leep (a.k.a. Mullet Fingers), and finds himself drawn into an ecological controversy. When the owners of Mother Paula's Pancake House pick as its new location a nesting site for an endangered species of owl, Mullet Fingers goes into action, planting poisonous snakes on the construction site, putting alligators in the portable potties, and moving grading stakes to thwart the builders. In this environmentally friendly tale, Hiassen creates quirky characters that belong nowhere but in the Florida landscape he creates—especially Roy, whose sarcastic humor captures the realities of adolescence perfectly.

Focus Lesson 1: Establishing a Tone

PICTURE BOOK

I Am the Dog, I Am the Cat
Donald Hall
Barry Moser, illustrator

Think About the Writer's Work:

• Did he make the primary voice of his writing clear? (For example, happy, frustrated, knowledgeable, scared, convincing)

• Did he vary the tone from the beginning to the end?

• Was he expressive?

• Did he show that he cares about this topic?

Lesson Focus:

This extended free-verse poem alternates between a cat and a dog's point of view, providing a strong sense of what makes the two animals fundamentally different. The Rottweiler uses short, declarative sentences and strong verbs, creating a tone that is authoritative, stalwart, and forthright. The tabby, however, uses longer, more complex sentences and less forceful words, creating a more languid tone. In this lesson, students write their own poem in the same tones that Hall establishes in *I Am the Dog, I Am the Cat*.

Materials:

- a copy of *I Am the Dog, I Am the Cat*
- projection and copies of the Think About the Writer's Work questions above
- projections of selected illustrations and passages
- paper, pens, pencils

What to Do:

1. Divide the class into two groups. Assign one group "dog," the other "cat." Give each group five minutes to brainstorm words or general characteristics they associate with their animal.

2. Compile a list of students' words and general characteristics on the whiteboard. If students think of more items as you write, add them.

3. Compare the lists. Ask students to choose one or two words or general characteristics that best match a dog and a cat. For instance, they might choose *friendly* and *loveable* for the dog, and *aloof* and *self-centered* for the cat.

4. Read *I Am the Dog, I Am the Cat* to students, showing the illustrations and text by using a document camera, if possible. As they listen, ask students to continue jotting down words that describe dogs or cats.

5. Add the new words to the two class lists. Discuss the ways in which Hall establishes a specific tone for each animal. Ask students if they noticed similarities and differences in the verbs the dog and cat use (the dog uses more strong verbs). Ask them to compare the types of sentences the dog and cat use (short and declarative vs. longer and more complex). Ask students to explain how Hall's choice of verbs and sentence types helps establish the tone of each animal.

6. Give students a copy of the Think About the Writer's Work questions to refer to as they write. Ask students to pick either the dog or the cat and, in the voice of that character, write a letter of introduction to the producers of the fictional reality show, "Best Pet in All the Land" to land a spot on an upcoming episode. Remind students to use their Think About the Writer's Work questions to establish a tone that is in keeping with the dog and the cat from Hall's book.

7. Ask students from another class to listen to the letters and vote on the one with the most consistent tone, the one with the most convincing message, and the writer-pet who should win the coveted title of "Best Pet in All the Land."

Lesson Extension:

Put students into pairs and ask them to create a mock Facebook page for either the dog or the cat from the Hall book. The content and tone of their pages should be in keeping with those from the book.

Focus Lesson 2: Conveying the Purpose

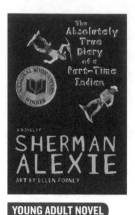

YOUNG ADULT NOVEL

The Absolutely True Diary of a Part-Time Indian
Sherman Alexie

Think About the Writer's Work:

- Is the purpose of his writing clear?

- Does his point of view come through?

- Is this the right tone for this kind of writing?

- Has he used strong voice throughout this piece?

Lesson Focus:

Arnold Spirit, or "Junior" as he's more commonly known, is a Native American teen who is doing his best to make it through life after suffering "water on the brain" as a child. A gifted cartoonist, he draws his way through humorous and tragic situations, sorting out where he belongs and what matters most. In this lesson, students hear poignant passages about the death of Junior's dog and about how old his textbooks are. Although both passages cast a light on the poverty in which Junior lives, each has a distinct tone. Students illustrate their take on the concept of the poverty in Alexie's style. From there, they match it to a song lyric so that readers appreciate and feel the impact of Junior's struggle through heartbreak, tragedy, and hopelessness.

Materials:

- a copy of *The Absolutely True Diary of a Part-Time Indian*

- projection and copies of the Think About the Writer's Work questions above

- projections of several illustrations from the book

- music CDs or access to online music stores such as iTunes or Rhapsody

- paper, pens, pencils

- projection of the following passage from the chapter entitled "Why Chicken Means So Much to Me":

> "He's really sick, Mom." I said. "He's going to die if we don't take him to the doctor."
>
> She looked hard at me. And her eyes weren't dark anymore, so I knew that she was going to tell me the truth. And trust me, there are times then the *last thing* you want to know is the truth.
>
> "Junior, sweetheart," Mom said. "I'm sorry, but we don't have any money for Oscar."
>
> "I'll pay you back," I said. "I promise."
>
> "Honey, it'll cost hundreds of dollars, maybe a thousand."
>
> "I'll pay back the doctor. I'll get a job."
>
> Mom smiled all sad and hugged me hard.
>
> Jeez, how stupid was I? What kind of job can a reservation Indian boy get? I was too young to deal blackjack at the casino, there were only about fifteen green grass lawns on the reservation and none of their owners outsourced the mowing jobs, and the only paper route was owned by a tribal elder named Wally. And he had to deliver only fifty papers, so his job was more like a hobby.
>
> There was nothing I could do to save Oscar.
>
> Nothing.
>
> Nothing.
>
> Nothing.
>
> Nothing.
>
> So I lay down on the floor beside him and patted his head and whispered his name for hours.
>
> Then Dad came home from wherever and had one of those long talks with Mom, and they decided something *without me.*
>
> And then Dad pulled down his rifle and bullets from the closet.

- projection of the following passage from the chapter entitled "Because Geometry Is Not a Country Somewhere Near France":

> But my lips and I stopped short when I saw this written on the inside front cover:
>
> **This Book Belongs to Agnes Adams**
>
> Okay, now you're probably asking yourself, "Who is Agnes Adams?"
>
> Well, let me tell you. Agnes Adams is my mother. MY MOTHER! And Adams is her *maiden* name.
>
> So that means my mother was born an Adams and she was still an Adams when she wrote her name in that book. And she was thirty when she gave birth to me. Yep, so that means I was staring at a geometry book that was at least thirty years older than I was.
>
> I couldn't believe it.
>
> How horrible is that?
>
> My school and my tribe are so poor and sad that we have to study from the same danged books our parents studied from. That is absolutely the saddest thing in the world.
>
> And let me tell you, that old, old, old, *decrepit* geometry book hit my heart with the force of a nuclear bomb. My hopes and dreams floated up in a mushroom cloud. What do you do when the world has declared nuclear war on you?

What to Do:

1. Share the Think About the Writer's Work questions with students and discuss how writing with a clear purpose enables us to connect with the reader in a meaningful way.

2. Tell students you are going to read two passages from *The Absolutely True Diary of a Part-Time Indian* by Sherman Alexie. Tell them that Alexie uses a variety of tones in his work, from hopeless to humorous, to help readers understand and connect with his story.

3. Project the first passage, read it aloud, and ask students to describe its tone. They may say it is sad, tragic, and/or heartbreaking. Ask them the purpose Alexie may have had for writing the book and to point out where Alexie clearly conveys that purpose in the passage. If students answer by saying that Junior is sad about losing his dog, ask them to think more deeply and ask themselves whether losing his dog might represent something even bigger.

4. Project the second passage and follow the same procedure as in step #3.

5. Ask students if Alexie's purpose is the same in both passages. Then ask them to describe the purpose that both pieces have in common: to illustrate the effects of poverty. Next, ask students to describe the tone in the second passage, which is angry and conveys hopelessness differently from the first passage.

6. Ask students to use their Think About the Writer's Work questions to probe their reactions to Alexie's writing and to consider whether they think knowing his purpose for writing contributes to the voice.

7. Put students into groups of three or four and ask them to draw a picture depicting poverty. When they've finished, have them add a caption or dialogue, the way Alexie does in his book. Be sure students draw upon their own voices, though. Ask them to find a song that matches their purpose for writing. Play the songs as students read and explain their work.

Lesson Extension:

Share passages from the book that have a more humorous tone than those used in the lesson. Ask students how varying the tone in a book can make the purpose of the writing even clearer than using only one, steady tone throughout.

Focus Lesson 3: Creating a Connection to the Audience

YOUNG ADULT NOVEL

Rules
Cynthia Lord

Think About the Writer's Work:

• Has she thought about the reader?

• Is this the right voice for the audience?

• Has she shown what matters most to her in this piece?

• Will the reader know how the author thinks and feels about the topic?

Lesson Focus:

Twelve-year-old Catherine doesn't know what to do about her autistic little brother, David. She loves him, but having him around makes her feel different from other kids her age. In an attempt to turn chaos into order, and improve the quality of life for herself and her brother, Catherine gives David a list of rules to live by, such as "no toys in the fish tank." In this lesson, students create their own list of rules to help them sort out the highs and lows of teenage life.

Materials:

- a copy of *Rules*

- projection and copies of the Think About the Writer's Work questions above

- paper, pens, pencils

- projection of "Rules for David," which appears at the start of the book:

RULES FOR DAVID

Chew with your mouth closed.
Say "thank you" when someone gives you a present (even if you don't like it).
If someone says "hi," you say "hi" back.
When you want to get out of answering something, distract the questioner with another question.
Not everything worth keeping has to be useful.
If the bathroom door is closed, knock (especially if Catherine has a friend over)!
Sometimes people laugh when they like you. But sometimes they laugh to hurt you.
No toys in the fish tank.

What to Do:

1. Summarize the story for students. Explain one of Lord's central points: Although living with a person with a disability such as autism can be challenging, family members can learn a great deal about life from him or her. Ask students to read about autism and its many forms by finding articles in the library, researching on the Internet, or interviewing medical personnel in the community. Discuss what they discover.

2. In *Rules*, Catherine creates a list of rules for David to help him navigate everyday life. Project the rules, read each one, and ask students to comment on why they think Catherine may have chosen to include it.

3. Put students into pairs and have them think of several rules that would help one or both of them in their everyday lives. The rules can be simple, such as "always lock the door at night," or complicated, such as "always tell your mom you think the dinner tastes good, even when it doesn't." Remind them to refer to the Think About the Writer's Work questions and apply them to their own thinking as they write.

4. Ask students to share their rules with another pair of classmates and discuss them. Have them revise any rules that classmates didn't understand or thought were inappropriate. Ask partners to share their rules with the whole class, if they wish. Comment on those that create the strongest connection to the audience.

5. Ask partners to come up with two rules that would make everyday life in the classroom easier.

6. When they've finished, have all students share their rules with the class, compile a list, and post it in the classroom for all to read and review regularly.

Lesson Extension:

Ask students to compile a list of rules to follow when they encounter a person with a disability. Encourage them to be honest so they create a connection to the disabled person.

Focus Lesson 4: Taking Risks to Create Voice

PICTURE BOOK

This Is Your Life Cycle
Heather Lynn Miller
Michael Chesworth, illustrator

Think About the Writer's Work:

• Has she used out-of-the-ordinary words?

• Is her writing interesting, fresh, and original?

• Has she tried to make her writing sound like her own?

• Has she tried something different from other authors?

Lesson Focus:

Take a complex process such as the life cycle of a dragonfly, add in Dahlia, a spunky main character on the brink of adulthood, wrap it all up in a game-show format (complete with commercials), and you have a piece of science writing with so much voice it is bound to become a classroom favorite. In this lesson, students explore how to write nonfiction in a voice that makes the information not only clear to the reader but also enjoyable to learn.

Materials:

• a copy of *This Is Your Life Cycle*

• projection and copies of the Think About the Writer's Work questions above

• projections of selected pages

• paper, pens, pencils

What to Do:

1. Show students the cover of *This Is Your Life Cycle* and ask if they have studied life cycles in science class. Most will respond they have. Briefly discuss the topic to get a grasp on their understanding of it.

2. Ask students if they have ever watched a game show on TV. Most will respond they have. Briefly discuss a few of their favorites and why they like them.

3. Project the Think About the Writer's Work questions and explain that sometimes writers create voice by taking risks—or by doing something completely original and unexpected. Tell them you are going to share a book by an author who did just that by taking a serious topic (the life cycle) and writing about it in a completely original and unexpected way (in a game-show format).

4. Read the book and share the illustrations using a document camera, if you have access to one. Otherwise, face the pages toward the class.

5. After reading, give students time to talk in small groups about the book and make a list of three "risks" Miller takes to create voice. These may include using first-person narrative, using a game-show format, using dialogue, including commercials, personifying insects and other animals, and so on. When they've finished, have them call out risks. List them on the whiteboard.

6. Ask students, working in the same small groups, to think of a product that a character in the book might use, such as the life-cycle alarm clock, the perfect prom dress for a "white wiggling dryad," strap-on wings for the dragonfly nymph, or junk food for grubs.

7. Tell students to create an advertisement for their product, using as much voice as possible. Remind them to refer to the Think About the Writer's Work questions as they write. Also, encourage them to illustrate their advertisements to add interest and detail. When they've finished, have them share their work with the class.

Lesson Extension:

Assign characters from *This Is Your Life Cycle* to students. Ask them to perform the narrative by reading their lines from the book with as much expression as possible. Discuss how the book's playful format and serious content work together to create strong voice.

CHAPTER 4

Word Choice

"The craft of writing itself can be inspiring. It is intoxicating to play around with language, to hear the music of what we say, to see more clearly as we speak, to follow the unexpected paths where words take us.**"**

—DONALD MURRAY from *A Writer Teaches Writing*

The path to using words well can be a long and twisted one. Young writers tend to produce drafts that are chock-full of imprecise and repetitive words. During revision, they sometimes cast aside perfect words in favor of longer, more complex ones designed to impress. It's only through continued revision that young writers learn to choose perfect words, to craft stunning sentences from those words, and to delight their readers as a result.

Great books can teach how to use words. Take *To Kill a Mockingbird*, for example. Even if we've never been to a small, rural Southern community, we feel as if we have after experiencing Harper Lee's careful attention to how people speak, their social customs, and the details of everyday life. On the other hand, in *Motel of the Mysteries*, David Macaulay uses words to create a scientific, deliberately ponderous tone. In *The Blue Star*, Tony Earley's words help us get inside the main character's head and suffer, right along with him, the sweet agony of a first crush. The lessons writers teach us about word choice are as varied as their books.

But those lessons are there, lying between two covers, waiting to be learned.

Words are like building blocks. By carefully selecting nouns, verbs, adjectives, adverbs, and every other kind of word, writers construct a message. If that message is solid, the words spark the imagination, create images, and connect—on many levels—with readers. Good word choice brings clarity to the writer's ideas. It also supports organization, since words signal sequence (*then, later, while*) and transitions (*however, furthermore, therefore*), creating a logical flow. It also creates voice, as William Zinsser asserts: "Good writing has an aliveness that keeps the reader reading from one paragraph to the next, and it's not a question of 'gimmicks' to personalize the author. It's a question of using the English language in a way that will achieve the greatest clarity and strength" (1976, pp. 5–6). Word choice is the workhorse trait: It's how writers transform the ordinary into the extraordinary, the mundane into the spectacular. It's how they use language to move, enlighten, and inspire. To accomplish all this, writers must embrace the key qualities of the word choice trait:

✴ **Applying Strong Verbs**
The writer uses many "action words," giving the piece punch and pizzazz. He or she has stretched to find lively verbs that add energy to the piece.

✴ **Selecting Striking Words and Phrases**
The writer uses many finely honed words and phrases. His or her creative and effective use of literary techniques such as alliteration, similes, and metaphors makes the piece a pleasure to read.

✴ **Using Specific and Accurate Words**
The writer uses words with precision. He or she selects words the reader needs in order to fully understand the message. The writer chooses nouns, adjectives, adverbs, and so forth that create clarity and bring the topic to life.

✴ **Choosing Words That Deepen Meaning**
The writer uses words to capture the reader's imagination and enhance the piece's meaning. There is a deliberate attempt to choose the best word over the first word that comes to mind.

Middle school writers need to fall in love with words and go where those words take them. When they hear the extraordinary language of mentor texts, they will want to create that language themselves. And who better to inspire young writers than the master wordsmiths selected for this chapter?

Mentor Texts in This Chapter

Applying Strong Verbs
Romeow and Drooliet, Laden
Twelve Rounds to Glory: The Story of Muhammad Ali, Smith, Jr.
Skulduggery Pleasant, Landy
The Green Futures of Tycho, Sleator
The Blue Star, Earley
To Kill a Mockingbird, Lee

Selecting Striking Words and Phrases
Spuds, Hesse
When I Heard the Learn'd Astronomer, Whitman
Everything on a Waffle, Horvath
Cinnamon Girl, Herrera
The Hunger Games, Collins
A Wizard of Earthsea, Le Guin

Using Specific and Accurate Words
Americans Who Tell the Truth, Shetterly
The Dinosaurs of Waterhouse Hawkins, Kerley
Because of Winn-Dixie, DiCamillo
Becoming Naomi León, Ryan
The Last Book in the Universe, Philbrick
Waiting for Normal, Connor

Choosing Words That Deepen Meaning
Motel of the Mysteries, Macaulay
A Seed Is Sleepy, Aston
The Skirt, Soto
The Misadventures of Benjamin Bartholomew Piff: Wishful Thinking, Lethcoe
Uglies, Westerfeld
Letters From Rifka, Hesse

Key Quality: Applying Strong Verbs

Romeow and Drooliet
Nina Laden, author and illustrator
Chronicle Books, 2005

Nina Laden elevates the term "puppy love" to new heights in this parody of Shakespeare's legendary tragedy. Romeow Felini, a cat, is not like his brothers who enjoy climbing trees, chasing birds, and remaining loyal to the family. He's got bigger fish to fry—especially when it comes to romance. So when he spots the dazzling Drooliet Barker, a dog, at a costume ball hosted by her family, he falls hopelessly in love with her... and she with him. After a short courtship, the unlikely couple sneaks off to marry. And when their families find out, as you might expect, the fur flies. Use this book not only to introduce your students to Shakespeare's plays, but also to expose them to one writer's exquisite use of verbs, as proven in the book's final moment: "Now stories will come and stories will go. Some wither and die. Some blossom and grow. Some live in your heart. So don't you forget the tale of Romeow and Drooliet."

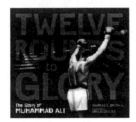

Twelve Rounds to Glory: The Story of Muhammad Ali
Charles R. Smith Jr.
Bryan Collier, illustrator
Candlewick Press, 2007

"Float like a butterfly, sting like a bee..." That's just what Muhammad Ali did in the ring with his body and what Charles R. Smith Jr. does in this book with his words. Smith gives us the full picture of Ali's life, from his birth as Cassius Clay in Louisville, Kentucky, and his encounters with racism during childhood, to his historic fights with Sonny Liston and Joe Frazier, to his decision to change his name for religious reasons, to his rejection of the Vietnam War as a conscientious objector, and finally to his lighting of the Olympic torch in 1996, hands shaking from Parkinson's Disease but pride burning as brightly as the flame itself. That said, this is more than a standard biography. It is pure poetry. Smith's rap-style language lifts off the page, weaving and bobbing and jabbing with championship force. *Twelve Rounds to Glory* delivers a one-two punch by teaching students about a great athlete *and* the craft of writing.

Skulduggery Pleasant

Derek Landy
HarperCollins, 2008

Twelve-year-old Stephanie Edgely has
recently inherited three things: her Uncle
Gordon's mansion, a supernatural friend,
and a murder mystery to solve. Skulduggery
Pleasant, a skeleton being, saves Stephanie's
life on her first night in the mansion. From
there, they become inseparable and try to
solve the mystery of her uncle's murder,
which may have to do with arch villain Nefarian Serpine, who
is looking for an ancient scepter that will pave the way to world
domination. Derek Landy creates a world unknown to human kind,
one where magic and the fight between good and evil coexist.
Readers will love Skulduggery, Stephanie, and their potent detective
partnership. Strong verbs keep them hopping as they chase down the
villains. This book is a little bit Harry Potter, a little bit Indiana Jones,
and a little bit Philip Marlowe.

The Green Futures of Tycho

William Sleator
Elsevier/Dutton, 1981

While planting zucchini and tomatoes in his
backyard, eleven-year-old Tycho Tithonus
digs up something much more valuable than
dirt: a small, metal object left there millions
of years ago by aliens. When Tycho discovers
that the object is a time-traveling device,
he uses it to get even with his older brothers and sister—and
learns the hard way that altering the future can be very dangerous.
Tycho meets different troubling versions of himself, each created by his own shortsighted
actions. Sleator is adept at taking real science and speculating on the consequences of using
it unwisely. In this case, the youngest child in a strange family finds that the power he holds
is best left untouched. The precarious situation in which Tycho finds himself is superbly
captured through Sleator's use of action words.

Questions to Ask When Choosing Books

When browsing the bookstore
or library for books to use when
teaching about word choice, ask
yourself:

- Does the book contain vivid
  "action words"—for example,
  scurry rather than *run*? Do
  those words give the writing
  punch and pizzazz?

- Has the author chosen words
  that sound just right? Does
  he or she use compound
  adjectives, alliteration,
  onomatopoeia, and other
  literary techniques?

- Will the words help my
  students create pictures in
  their minds? Or are they more
  likely to confuse them? Has the
  author chosen the best words
  possible for the grade I teach?
  For the subjects I teach?

- Is there evidence that the
  author really thought about
  the words he or she selected?
  Will those words capture
  my students' imagination and
  engage them in the text?

The Blue Star

Tony Earley
Little, Brown, 2008

FOCUS LESSON: Page 85 Jim Glass is a high school senior at Aliceville School in rural North Carolina. As World War II looms on the horizon, the people of his Appalachian community assume their stations in life—some are mountain people, some are farmers, and some are one step away from being slaves. Although Chrissie Steppe is the girl of Jim's dreams, she has agreed to wed Bucky Bucklaw upon his return from the war, for all the wrong reasons. Chrissie is treated like a second-class citizen in more than one way, being not only poor but also of Native American heritage, and Jim's hopes for her are surely challenged because of her difficult situation. He will have to navigate the complications that life unfairly presents. In this sequel to *Jim the Boy*, Tony Earley paints an accurate and charming picture of the Appalachian culture in the 1940s. And his use of strong verbs captures agrarian life and the characters' actions well.

To Kill a Mockingbird

Harper Lee
J.B. Lippincott & Co, 1960

In Depression-era Alabama, six-year-old Scout tells the story of how her father, Atticus, provides legal defense for Tom Robinson, an African-American man accused of raping an impoverished young white woman. Scout describes every person and event with great accuracy and detail, even though the alleged crime took place long before the time the story is set. Scout's memories of her brother, Jem; Calpurnia, the family cook and babysitter; Dill, a neighbor boy who is visiting from Mississippi; Mayella and Bob Ewell, Tom's ignorant, racist accusers; Heck Tate, the town sheriff; Miss Maudie Atkinson, their elderly friend; the mysterious Boo Radley; and other colorful characters paint a precise depiction of the South just before World War II. Timeless issues that confront society, such as race relations, poverty, and peer pressure, are thoughtfully addressed. Lee's carefully chosen verbs help define characters' personality traits—their fear, their shyness, their gentility, and so forth. (Mature Themes)

Key Quality: Selecting Striking Words and Phrases

Spuds
Karen Hesse
Wendy Watson, illustrator
Scholastic, 2008

If you travel our great nation, you'll learn that everyone doesn't speak English the same way. Each region has its own dialect—its unique version of English, with its own grammar, syntax, vocabulary, and pronunciation rules—that is passed along from generation to generation. Good fiction writers know this and apply it to their work. They not only place their characters in a setting, they give them the language of that setting. Take *Spuds*, for example, the story of three impoverished siblings who pilfer a neighbor's potato field one night, only to return home with stones that, in the darkness, they mistook for potatoes. Interestingly, Hesse does not reveal the setting, but we can only suspect the Deep South with passages like, "We left the road and stole into Kenney's field, creepin' over the clawed-up earth, our hands feelin' for night spuds." A heartwarming story about the power of forgiveness, crackling with striking words and phrases.

When I Heard the Learn'd Astronomer
Walt Whitman
Loren Long, illustrator
Simon & Schuster, 2004

If you're like most middle school teachers we know, you'll agree—getting kids excited about nineteenth-century American poetry ain't easy. The mere mention of Emily Dickinson, John Greenleaf Whittier, or Henry Wadsworth Longfellow triggers a collective yawn. But when that poetry is brought to life in a picture book, the impact can be powerful. The illustrations help students translate tricky language and see beauty in it. They support students in their effort to understand what the writer is trying to tell them. In this interpretation of a Walt Whitman poem, Loren Long's illustrations do just that. The poem's "I" is a young boy who attends a very adult astronomy lecture and, understandably, winds up "tired and sick." Afterwards, he wanders into "the mystical moist night-air." As he ponders the sky, looking up "in perfect silence at the stars," he is overwhelmed by its beauty. He begins to think and wonder like a future "learn'd astronomer."

Everything on a Waffle

Polly Horvath
Farrar, Straus and Giroux, 2001

Eleven-year-old Primrose Squarp lost her parents in a storm at sea, according to the townsfolk of Coal Harbour, British Columbia. But Primrose isn't the type to be ruled by the opinions of others and believes her parents are still alive. For the time being, however, Primrose is put in temporary custody of Miss Perfidy, who doesn't like children and smells strongly of mothballs. When the Navy reassigns Primrose's Uncle Jack to Coal Harbour, he takes over as guardian. But in Primrose's estimation, her real guardian is Kate Bowzer, owner of a small restaurant where everything is served on a waffle. People come and go at surprising speed in Coal Harbour, but Primrose regards it all with a wry sense of humor and wise observations about life. Horvath brings Primrose to life through striking word choice, even in the recipes.

Cinnamon Girl: Letters Found Inside a Cereal Box

Juan Felipe Herrera
Rayo, 2005

After experiencing tragic events and bad circumstances in a small Midwestern town, thirteen-year-old Yolanda and her family have recently joined Puerto Rican relatives on the Lower East Side of Manhattan. When the 9/11 attack on the World Trade Center leaves her uncle in a coma, Yolanda promises to gather dust from the explosion and return it to Ground Zero in a symbolic attempt to bring comfort to all the victims and their families. However, she has a tendency to befriend and follow the wrong people, and she finds herself headed for trouble one night. Told in letters and poems, *Cinnamon Girl* unfolds in English, Spanish, and Spanglish. Like many multilingual authors, Juan Felipe Herrera chooses the best words for the feelings he wants to communicate, drawing from all three languages. In doing so, he creates a memorable account of the aftereffects of the 9/11 tragedy.

The Hunger Games

Suzanne Collins
Scholastic, 2008

FOCUS LESSON: Page 87 In a post-apocalyptic land called Panem, the Capitol rules over thirteen districts, each providing some form of goods or services. In the coal mining district, District 12, Katniss lives a somewhat subversive life, hunting illegally in the forbidden wilderness and supplying her mother and younger sister with more food than the meager allotment doled out by the Capitol. In order to distract citizens from their tragic lives and keep them in their place, the Capitol holds the annual Hunger Games, a televised competition in which 24 tributes—12 teenage boys and 12 teenage girls picked by lottery from each district—fight to the death. The games require all the martial skills and mental dexterity that Katniss has developed as a hunter. A little bit Roman history, a little bit reality television, and a little bit Super Bowl, this book is a spellbinder with a language all its own. (Mature Themes)

A Wizard of Earthsea
Ursula K. Le Guin
Parnassus, 1968

Duny is a resident of Gont, where dragons pose a threat, and good and evil battle for supremacy. When Duny's natural talent for magic saves his home village, Ogion, a wise old magician, makes him an apprentice and nicknames him Sparrowhawk. Sparrowhawk turns out to be undisciplined and impatient, so Ogion sends him off to the wizards' school on the Isle of Roke. At the school, he attempts spells far beyond his level and unwittingly summons and releases a dangerous creature from the dark side. Sparrowhawk leaves Roke to right the wrongs he and others have created. In the process, he encounters many creatures, including the one he set free, whose fate winds up being tied to his. This book, the first in a series of three, is tightly written and contains invented terminology that is sure to intrigue readers.

Key Quality: Using Specific and Accurate Words

Americans Who Tell the Truth
Robert Shetterly, author and illustrator
Dutton Children's Books, 2005

In this collection of powerful statements from 50 of America's most influential thinkers, Robert Shetterly provides hope for the post-9/11 generation. Although they represent a range of cultural backgrounds, speak various languages, and come from a variety of fields, the people Shetterly quotes have one purpose: upholding democracy by revealing the truth behind government actions—and celebrating those actions when they're honorable and challenging them when they're not. What they say, at times, is controversial. In fact, their words are so pointed, they will undoubtedly spark debate. But that's precisely what makes this book an invaluable teaching tool. Share it with your students to get them contemplating their own beliefs about what makes America great. The biographical sketches at the back of the book provide useful starting points for students interested in pursuing more information on those profiled.

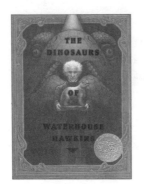

The Dinosaurs of Waterhouse Hawkins
Barbara Kerley
Brian Selznick, illustrator
Scholastic, 2001

The best nonfiction reads like fiction, as Barbara Kerley proves in this fascinating biography of Benjamin Waterhouse Hawkins, the nineteenth-century British sculptor who created full-sized models of dinosaurs with paleontologist Richard Owen. Using unearthed parts of skeletons to estimate their size and shape, Owen designed extraordinary creatures—the iguanodon, the megalosaurus, and the haylaeosaurus, among others—while Hawkins brought them as close to life as possible, using stone, wire, clay, cement, and paint. With the support of Queen Victoria, his models were put on public display at London's Crystal Palace in 1854, catapulting him to international fame. From there, Hawkins went to America to continue his work, where he experienced remarkable success and unfathomable heartbreak. Although the book is loaded with scientific terms, don't let it scare you. This is the thinking child's *Jurassic Park*.

Because of Winn-Dixie
Kate DiCamillo
Candlewick, 2000

"I know I don't need a dog. But this dog needs me," Opal tells her father after rescuing a big, ugly, smelly, starving, but friendly mutt from the Winn-Dixie grocery store in their new hometown of Naomi, Florida. Opal's father, a minister, was abandoned by his wife seven years earlier. Opal is lonely and confused about her mother's absence. In the end, she needs the dog, which she names Winn-Dixie, just as much as he needs her. Winn-Dixie has a knack for attracting serendipitous friends to Opal, including Opal's own father. The dog also becomes Opal's confidant, as she talks out all the things in life she doesn't understand, such as her mother's departure. Telling the story from Opal's perspective, DiCamillo uses just the right words throughout the book.

Becoming Naomi León
Pam Muñoz Ryan
Scholastic, 2004

FOCUS LESSON: Page 88 Although Naomi Soledad León Outlaw, her brother Clive, and the grandmother who is raising them don't have much more than their trailer, resting in Avocado Acres Trailer Rancho, in Lemon Tree, California, they are a stable and happy family. Then Naomi and Clive's alcoholic mother, who now calls herself Skyla, returns out of nowhere to claim Naomi, but not Clive. Gram knows that all Skyla wants is welfare money and the free babysitting Naomi will provide for her new boyfriend's children, so Gram takes off with the kids to find their father in Oaxaca, Mexico. Mr. León is an artist who carves animals from wood. Naomi is a talented carver as well. As the trip rolls along, Gram teaches the kids about their Mexican heritage. But will she have the legal means to prevent Skyla from removing Naomi from the only family she has ever known? Ryan's words describe people and things with great charm and accuracy.

The Last Book in the Universe
Rodman Philbrick
Scholastic, 2000

In this post-apocalyptic science fiction novel, Philbrick's two protagonists, Spaz and Ryter, live in a time when gated communities are inhabited by genetically enhanced aristocrats and burned-out city blocks are run by gangs, or "bangers," headed by urban warlords. No one reads or writes; in fact, books are a thing of the past. Virtual, out-of-body experiences are available through the insertion of "mindprobe" needles that send electrical impulses directly to the brain to simulate the real thing. Although Spaz initially believes Ryter is a typical "gummy," an elderly person, he learns that Ryter is actually a "writer," a recorder of the world's stories. As he and Spaz embark on an important quest, he explains everything about books to Spaz, who in the end takes over the role of writer, and creates "the last book in the universe." The most accurate words in this book may very well be in the slang Philbrick has created, such as "provs" for genetically improved people and "gummies" for elderly people who have lost their teeth.

Waiting for Normal
Leslie Connor
Katherine Tegen Books, 2008

Twelve-year-old Addie loves her stepfather, Dwight, but her mother, Mommers, doesn't, and eventually leaves him. After the divorce, Addie winds up in a trailer in Schenectady, New York, and her half-sisters wind up in a beautiful bed-and-breakfast upstate. Even though Mommers has mental health issues that prevent her from being a good parent, Addie is remarkably self-reliant and positive. She makes the most of things, even acknowledging when she has "faked a big old smile" to keep the adults around her from feeling guilty. In that spirit, she creates her own surrogate family with Soula, a breast cancer patient, and Elliot, a gay man, who run the gas station/convenience store next door. Connor creates a vivid, believable world inhabited by equally vivid, believable characters whose personalities are revealed through their actions. Her word choice, especially in dialogue, has pinpoint accuracy. This is a touching novel, artfully constructed.

Key Quality: Choosing Words That Deepen Meaning

Word Choice

Motel of the Mysteries
David Macaulay, author and illustrator
Houghton Mifflin Company, 1979

FOCUS LESSON: Page 90

The *New York Times* called *Motel of the Mysteries* "a marvel of imagination," and it's easy to see why. Macaulay jettisons us 2000 years into the future for an expedition to "Usa," an ancient, subterranean country formerly known as the U.S.A. There, amateur archeologist Howard Carson stumbles onto "a tomb"—or, more accurately, a motel. A run-of-the-mill motel. Yet Carson finds it astounding and attaches all kinds of harebrained significance to the "treasures" he finds. He labels a television set "the great altar," toilet paper "sacred parchment," an overflowing room-service tray "a sacrificial meal offered to the gods of eternal life." Macaulay chooses his words so carefully, and illustrates them so magnificently with his pen-and-ink drawings, readers can't help but be swept into the miraculously mundane world he creates. This is satire at its finest.

A Seed Is Sleepy
Diane Hutts Aston
Sylvia Long, illustrator
Chronicle Books, 2007

When was the last time you picked up an information book that read like poetry? Most likely not recently, since writers of those books tend to focus more on content than craft. Aston, however, gives equal attention to both in this follow-up to her celebrated *An Egg Is Quiet*. The detail-packed format is simple. Aston devotes nearly every page spread to a particular quality of a seed or group of seeds (sleepy, secretive, and adventurous, for example) and goes on to explain what she means by it. She also attaches helpful captions and notes to Sylvia Long's stunning illustrations, which burst from the page as if we're viewing the seeds through a magnifying glass. Aston and Long don't waste a page. They anticipate the reader's every question. Their book is a testament to the power of one word—how it can say a million things when the writer takes the time to choose it carefully and position it skillfully.

The Skirt

Gary Soto
Random House, 1992

While jumping from seat to seat on the bus to avoid flirtatious boys, Miata forgets all about her mother's treasured *folklórico* skirt, which she had taken to school to show to friends. As the bus drives out of sight on Friday afternoon, Miata knows that she must somehow retrieve the skirt by Sunday, for the dance at which she plans to wear it. Miata has two choices: She can admit her mistake to her parents and enlist their help to retrieve the skirt or she can keep her blunder a secret and attempt to retrieve the skirt herself, thereby sparing herself her parents' disapproval. What will she decide? Soto communicates the importance of tradition, friendship, and family relationships in dialogue that contains an authentic combination of English and a bit of Spanish. He uses language that goes to the heart of the matter.

The Misadventures of Benjamin Bartholomew Piff: Wishful Thinking

Jason Lethcoe
Grosset & Dunlap, 2007

When his parents are lost in an airplane accident, Benjamin Piff is sentenced to live in Pinch's Home for Wayward Boys. Ben is miserable there until, on his birthday, he asks for infinite wishes before blowing out the candles on his cake. He gets what he asks for, and life greatly improves at first. But eventually it creates chaos. The Wishworks, a paranormal enterprise that oversees all wishes, is suddenly in danger of a hostile takeover by the Curseworks, its evil counterpart. Ben must find a way to thwart the Curseworks' evil ambition. Partnering with Thomas Candlewick, Wishworks president, he begins his "misadventures." This story is much lighter than other good-versus-evil fantasies for young readers, such as the books in the Chronicles of Narnia and even the Harry Potter series. With characters named Wolfgang Warblegrunt and Leonardo Snifflewhiffle, and a plot that is delightfully implausible, Lethcoe's fantasy is a joy to read. His word choice enhances the reader's understanding of Bartholomew's experiences.

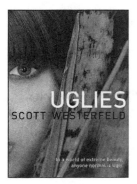

Uglies

Scott Westerfeld
Simon & Schuster, 2005

In Westerfeld's post-apocalyptic world, the population is divided into "uglies" and "pretties." Until the age of sixteen, people are "uglies." At 16, they are required to undergo an extensive operation that corrects every physical flaw, turning them into supermodels—or "pretties." Pretties reside on one side of the river, where they enjoy exciting social lives, while uglies live with their families on the other side of the river, where they do nothing much more than go to school. Life is too controlled and individuality too limited for some people, however, and a rebel camp out in the wilderness is home to a small group of resistance fighters who suspect there is more to the pretty operation than the public knows. Tally Youngblood is an ugly who is about to become a pretty. When she becomes a spy for the government, she infiltrates the rebel camp. Does she find what she was expecting to find there? Westerfeld packs meaning into every passage with his strong word choice. (Mature Themes)

Letters From Rifka

Karen Hesse
Penguin, 1992

As famine and poverty swept Russia during the first part of twentieth century, Jewish communities became the scapegoats for an incompetent government. As a result, pogroms, programs of organized abuse and genocide, swept the country. Hundreds of thousands of Jews fled to safer places. Through the character of Rifka, Hesse retells the story of her own family's escape from Europe to the United States, which began in September, 1919, and ended in October, 1920. Through letters, twelve-year-old Rifka describes multiple brushes with death, as she and her parents and two brothers make their way from the Ukraine to Poland, to Belgium, and finally to Ellis Island. Hesse's descriptions of Russian soldiers searching a train, the effects of typhus on the human body, and the frustration of being left behind because of ringworm bring to life a horrifying episode in world history. Hesse communicates Rifka's feelings, and enhances their meaning, through careful word choice.

Focus Lesson 1: Applying Strong Verbs

YOUNG ADULT NOVEL

The Blue Star
Tony Earley

Think About the Writer's Work:

- Has he used action words?

- Did he stretch to get a better word—*scurry* rather than *run*?

- Do his verbs give the writing punch and pizzazz?

- Did he avoid *is, am, are, was, were, be, being,* and *been* whenever he could?

Lesson Focus:

In *Jim the Boy*, readers met Jim, a ten-year-old who is a kind, considerate boy growing up with his mother and her brothers in rural North Carolina. In this sequel, Jim is a high school student experiencing new emotions about familiar people and places. Using strong verbs, Earley explains how Jim develops a "crush" on a girl who, until recently, he thought was just a friend. In this lesson, students explore how to use verbs to bring to life emotions of their own in their writing.

Materials:

- a copy of *The Blue Star*

- projection and copies of the Think About the Writer's Work questions above

- paper, pens, pencils

- projection and paper copies of the following passage from the chapter entitled "The History Lesson":

> Chrissie shifted in her seat, and the hair lying on Jim's history book moved slightly and became a small, glossy animal curled and napping in the sun. A muskrat, Jim thought. No, a mink. No, a small, black fox. A kit. Jim wondered if a kit fox would bite you if you tried to pet it. He placed his left hand on his history book and drummed his fingers. He slowly slid his fingers up the page toward Chrissie's hair. Chrissie shifted again. The kit twitched in its sleep, dreaming of green fields lush with mice. Jim stopped. He felt his heart stuttering beneath his skin. He pursed his lips and almost inaudibly whispered, "Shh." The kit remained still. He moved his hand up the slick paper, a line, a half line at a time, through the Yankee blockade, at Wilmington. Only the bravest blockade-running captains, under cover of darkness, were able to bring desperately needed supplies into the besieged port. Jim raised his middle finger and inched his hand forward until his finger was suspended above Chrissie's black hair. He took a deep breath. He lowered his finger and touched her hair as gently as he knew how to touch anything. He had never felt anything so soft.

What to Do:

1. Tell students that you are going to share a passage from a book that tells the story of a high school boy who lives in the rural South with his mother and uncles. Though his life is simple, it is filled with interesting people and events.

2. Explain that as you read, you want students to listen for the way Earley uses verbs. Share the Think About the Writer's Work questions and discuss the power of verbs to make a piece of writing clear.

3. Give students photocopies of the passage. As you read the passage, ask students to follow along and circle the verbs.

4. When you've finished reading, ask students to call out the verbs in the passage. List them on the whiteboard. When the list is complete, ask students to tell you which verbs are particularly powerful to them as readers. Circle those verbs.

5. Discuss the ways in which using strong verbs allows Earley to describe the emotions associated with infatuation, without explicitly naming how Jim feels as a "crush" or that he is "in love." Remind students to refer to the Think About the Writer's Work questions to guide their thinking about using strong verbs in writing.

6. Group students in pairs and ask them to select another emotion to write about, such as fear, courage, humor, anxiety, loneliness, or gratitude. Ask them to write 2 or 3 lines describing the emotion but not naming it with a label.

7. Have them underline the verb (or verbs) in each sentence, checking to make sure it is as strong as possible.

8. Invite volunteers to read their sentences aloud and see if classmates can guess the emotion being described. List on the board the verbs from each piece.

9. Instruct students to write down favorite verbs from the Earley passage and from their classmates' pieces and keep the list with other writing materials to consult as they draft and revise their own work.

Lesson Extension:

Discuss with students how Earley uses strong verbs to help make his writing memorable. Ask students to pick a favorite book or magazine and examine a paragraph for the writer's use of verbs. Make a list of those that are strong and those that could be revised. Write better verbs next to the weak ones.

Focus Lesson 2: Selecting Striking Words and Phrases

YOUNG ADULT NOVEL

The Hunger Games
Suzanne Collins

Think About the Writer's Work:

- Did she try to use words that sound "just right"?
- Did she try hyphenating several shorter words to make an interesting-sounding new word?
- Did she try putting words with the same sound together?
- When the piece is read aloud, are there at least one or two lovely moments?

Lesson Focus:

In this horrific tale set in the future, sixteen-year-old Katniss is thrust onto the national stage when she is selected as a "tribute" in the annual Hunger Games, a brutal ritual in which young people are pitted against one another in a fight to the death. To make matters even more disturbing, the ritual is televised for the public as a reality show. In this lesson, students explore how Collins applies striking words and phrases in just the right doses and in just the right places. From there, they create movie posters for the film version of *The Hunger Games*, based on the passage.

Materials:

- a copy of *The Hunger Games*
- projection and copies of the Think About the Writer's Work questions above
- paper, pens, pencils
- projection of the following passage from Chapter 11:

> Sixty seconds. That's how long we're required to stand on our metal circles before the sound of a gong releases us. Step off before the minute is up, and land mines blow your legs off. Sixty seconds to take in the ring of tributes, all equidistant from the Cornucopia, a giant golden horn shaped like a cone with a curved tail, the mouth of which is at least twenty feet high, spilling over with the things that will give us life here in the arena. Food, containers of water, weapons, medicine, garments, fire starters. Strewn around the Cornucopia are other supplies, their value decreasing the farther they are from the horn. For instance, only a few steps from my feet lies a three-foot square of plastic. Certainly it could be of some use in a downpour. But there in the mouth, I can see a tent pack that would protect from almost any sort of weather. If I had the guts to go in and fight for it against the other twenty-three tributes. Which I have been instructed not to do.
>
> We're on a flat, open stretch of ground. A plain of hard-packed dirt. Behind the tributes across from me, I can see nothing, indicating either a steep downward slope or even a cliff. To my right lies a lake. To my left and back, a sparse piney woods.

What to Do:

1. Summarize the plot of *The Hunger Games* for students. Ask if any of them has read *Fahrenheit 451* by Ray Bradbury, "The Lottery" by Shirley Jackson, or *The Giver* by Lois Lowry. Discuss why futuristic novels and stories like these are so enticing.

2. Tell students that *The Hunger Games* has particularly strong words and phrases, which enhances the reading experience by providing language that inspires, delights, and, in this case, terrifies. Project the Think About the Writer's Work with students and discuss it.

3. Project and read the passage. Ask students to close their eyes and visualize the place Katniss describes. As the passage is read, emphasize the words and phrases, "sound of a gong releases us," "a giant golden horn shaped like a cone with a curved tail," "A plain of hard-packed dirt," "a sparse piney woods."

4. Put students into pairs and ask them to design a poster advertising the movie version of *The Hunger Games*. The poster should include a picture of the setting Katniss describes and a few tantalizing lines about what is about to happen and why the reader *must* see the movie. Remind students to refer to the Think About the Writer's Work questions as they draw and write.

5. Have students share their posters with the class by explaining their pictures and reading their text. How clearly and compellingly did they capture Katniss's description? Will their posters entice moviegoers to see the film version of the book?

Lesson Extension:

Tell students, "Imagine you are Katniss. Using striking words and phrases, explain in writing how it feels to know you must kill other tributes in order to survive the Hunger Games."

Focus Lesson 3: Using Specific and Accurate Words

CHAPTER BOOK

Becoming Naomi León
Pam Muñoz Ryan
Target Trait: Word Choice

Think About the Writer's Work:

• Has she used nouns and modifiers that help the reader see a picture?

• Did she avoid using words that might confuse the reader?

• Did she use words that might pleasantly surprise the reader?

• Are these the most precise words she could have used?

Lesson Focus:

Naomi Soledad León Outlaw's life is complicated. She lives with her quirky but loveable grandmother and little brother Owen because her mother and father have left. Although Gran does her best to raise the children well, Naomi struggles with the fact that she wears clothes that are homemade, she has difficulty speaking up, and she lacks special skills or interests that would give her status in school. Naomi loves words, however, and keeps a notebook full of them. She uses her notebook to explore her feelings and find answers to some of her hardest life questions. In this lesson, students start their own "splendid words lists" and other lists, based on the ones Naomi keeps in her notebook.

Materials:

- a copy of *Becoming Naomi León*
- projection and copies of the Think About the Writer's Work questions above
- students' writer's notebook
- pens, pencils
- projection of the following passage from the chapter entitled "A Paddling of Ducks":

> Chewing on the end of my pencil, I got back to my list, which Gram said was one of the things I did best. I had all kinds of lists in my notebook, the shortest being "Things I am Good At" which consisted of 1) Soap carving, 2) Worrying, and 3) Making lists.
>
> There was my "Regular and Everyday Worries" list, which included 1) Gram was going to die because she was old, and 2) Owen would never be right, 3) I will forget something if I don't make a list, 4) I will lose my lists, and 5) Abominations. I made a list of splendid words, types of rocks, books I read, and unusual names. Not to mention the lists I had copied, including "Baby Animal Names," "Breeds of Horses," and my current favorite, "*Animal Groups from The Complete and Unabridged Animal Kingdom with over 200 Photographs.*"

What to Do:

1. Explain the story of *Becoming Naomi León*, emphasizing that the main character collects words in a notebook to deal with the many challenges her life presents.

2. Share the Think About the Writer's Work questions and discuss how learning to pay attention to specific and accurate words, as Naomi does in the story, can increase a writer's vocabulary and provide a wealth of word options when drafting and revising. Note that specific words should be used instead of more generic ones—for example "I ordered a diet cola" instead of "I ordered a soda." Accurate words refer to the use of words within content areas—for example "galaxy" instead of "bunch of stars."

3. Project the passage and ask students to follow along as you read it to them.

4. On the whiteboard, jot down the different kinds of lists that Naomi says she keeps.

5. Pass out the writer's notebooks and ask students to create three lists: Content Words, Accurate Words, and Splendid Words that can be words students like for any reason they wish.

6. Put students into pairs and have them brainstorm at least eight words for each list. Remind students to consult their Think About the Writer's Work questions as they consider words to add. Ask them to pick five words of each type—Accurate, Specific, and Splendid—and write them as a list under one of the three headings.

7. Put pairs together in small groups. Encourage them to share favorites from each list and change their lists if they hear new words or to think of new ones as they discuss.

8. Make a master list of all Accurate, Specific, and Splendid Words and post it so students can refer to it as they write to get ideas for specific and accurate words to use in their writing.

Lesson Extension:

Ask students to begin making subsets of words from their word lists classified by part of speech. Tell them to color code their words: red for verbs, green for nouns, blue for adjectives, and so on. As they are writing and need a particular type of word, they can use the color coding to help them find one quickly and efficiently.

Focus Lesson 4: Choosing Words That Deepen Meaning

PICTURE BOOK

Motel of the Mysteries
David Macaulay, author and illustrator

Think About the Writer's Work:

- Did he choose words that show he really thought about them?
- Did he avoid using the same words repeatedly?
- Do his words capture the reader's imagination?
- Has he found the best way to express himself?

Lesson Focus:

An archeologist from the future discovers a motel hidden beneath the earth's surface and catalogs all the common objects he finds, such as a remote control for a TV, a shower cap, and a sink stopper, assigning them scholarly yet far-fetched names and uses, since he is so clueless about their original purposes. In this lesson, students choose objects from the book, name them, and write descriptions of them using words and phrases similar to those used by Macaulay.

Materials:

- a copy of *Motel of the Mysteries*
- projection of the Think About the Writer's Work questions above
- projection of selected illustrations and passages
- paper, pens, pencils

What to Do:

1. Explain to students that you are going to share *Motel of the Mysteries* with them, a book that contains specific language to make the story interesting, provide information, and create the voice of the writing. Share that the author uses words to create a satire on archeology, religion, and culture.

2. Show students a copy of the Think About the Writer's Work questions and discuss why it is important to choose words carefully to make ideas clear.

3. Share the first section of the book, up to "The Treasures" and discuss the book's premise and the language Macaulay uses to explain it.

4. Ask students to think about Macaulay's words and the tone they create. Students will likely notice that the words are academic and overblown, and the language dense, creating a serious tone for a far-fetched idea.

5. Project or show the pages that number and name the objects Macaulay describes.

6. Project the page that contains the drawing of the woman wearing a toilet seat on her head, and ask students to call out other possible names and uses for the object. Tell them to use words that archeologist Howard Carson's team would use and compare their choices to Macaulay's.

7. Project the page showing the skeleton in the bathtub and other objects from that same scene, and repeat steps above, comparing students' ideas to Macaulay's.

8. Assign pairs of students one object that is described in the "Treasures" section of the book. Ask each pair to write a made-up description of the object and its use, using words to deepen the meaning and create a satirical tone similar to Macaulay's. Remind them to consider the Think About the Writer's Work questions as they write.

9. When they've finished, ask students to read their descriptions aloud to the class, while you project the drawing of the object. Compare their descriptions to Macaulay's. Read the epilogue on the final page of the book.

10. Ask students to discuss the relationship of words to the main idea Macaulay conveyed throughout *Motel of the Mysteries*.

Lesson Extension:

Ask students to walk around the school and select common objects such as lunchroom trays, basketballs, light switches. Have them draw the object, write a description of it, and explain how it is used from the point of view of an amateur archeologist such as Howard. Assemble the drawings and descriptions into a book like *Motel of the Mysteries*. Have students write an introduction and epilogue.

CHAPTER 5

Sentence Fluency

"Simplify, simplify. Thoreau said it, as we are so often reminded, and no American writer more consistently practiced what he preached. Open *Walden* to any page and you will find a man saying in a plain and orderly way what is on his mind:

'I went to the woods because I wished to live deliberately, to front only the essential facts of life, and see if I could not learn what it had to teach, and not, when I came to die, discover that I had not lived.'

How can the rest of us achieve such enviable freedom from clutter? The answer is to clear our heads of clutter. Clear thinking becomes clear writing; one can't exist without the other."

—WILLIAM ZINSSER from *On Writing Well*

Reading the mentor texts recommended in this chapter is like taking an advanced-placement course in sentence fluency. They're that good. Their sentences are free from clutter, artistically constructed, and grammatically spot-on. *The Music of Dolphins*, for example, begins simply, similar to Mila's life when she is taken away from the sea and her life with dolphins and learns English. Her sentences become increasingly complex, however, the more she learns about language and life as a human. At the end of the story, Mila decides to return to her life at sea—

and her sentences become simple again. Readers learn what it means to be human, in great measure, because of the sentence fluency used by the first person narrator, Mila, in this remarkable book.

Sentence fluency is about how words and phrases flow through a piece. It is achieved when the writer pays close attention to the way individual sentences are crafted and groups of sentences are combined.

Writing may seem like a silent act, but it isn't. When true writers read their drafts, they hear passages that sing out and those that don't. They check for natural starting and stopping points. They listen for the way the words sound as they flitter and flow within and among sentences. And when passages don't sing out, when starting and stopping points don't seem natural and words don't sound quite right, they know there is work to be done. They might weed out unnecessary words, vary the length and structure of sentences, or try a literary technique such as alliteration or assonance. That is why we call sentence fluency the auditory trait. True writers "read" for it with the ear as much as the eye. And they learn what writing should sound like from mentors.

Writing fluently is not easy because it requires the writer to conjure up everything he or she knows about language—how it works, how it looks, how it sounds, how it touches the person receiving it—in order to find the best approach for the piece. In other words, he or she must apply the following key qualities with skill and confidence:

✳ **Crafting Well-Built Sentences**

The writer carefully and creatively constructs sentences for maximum impact. Transition words such as *but*, *and*, and *so* are used successfully to join sentences and sentence parts.

✳ **Varying Sentence Types**

The writer uses various types of sentences (simple, compound, and/or complex) to enhance the central theme or story line. The piece is made up of an effective mix of long, complex sentences and short, simple ones.

✳ **Capturing Smooth and Rhythmic Flow**

The writer thinks about how the sentences sound. He or she uses phrasing that is almost musical. If the piece were read aloud, it would be easy on the ear.

✳ **Breaking the "Rules" to Create Fluency**

The writer diverges from standard English to create interest and impact. For example, he or she may use a sentence fragment, such as *All alone in the forest*, or a single word, such as *Bam!* to accent a particular moment or action. He or she might begin with informal words such as *well*, *and*, or *but* to create a conversational tone, or break rules intentionally to make dialogue sound authentic.

Mentor Texts in This Chapter

Crafting Well-Built Sentences

Owl Moon, Yolen

Old Turtle and the Broken Truth, Wood

The Jade Dragon, Marsden and Loh

Inkheart, Funke

Out of the Pocket, Konigsberg

Hippie Chick, Monninger

Varying Sentence Types

Morning on the Lake, Waboose

The Table Where Rich People Sit, Baylor

Shiloh, Naylor

Warrior Angel, Lipsyte

Tasting the Sky, Barakat

Does My Head Look Big in This? Abdel-Fattah

Capturing Smooth and Rhythmic Flow

Sitti's Secrets, Nye

Jazz ABZ: An A to Z Collection of Jazz Portraits, Marsalis

Football Genius, Green

A Single Shard, Park

Life, Love and the Pursuit of Free Throws, Rallison

The Face on the Milk Carton, Cooney

Breaking the "Rules" to Create Fluency

Show Way, Woodson

Once Upon a Cool Motorcycle Dude, O'Malley

When the Circus Came to Town, Horvath

The Music of Dolphins, Hesse

Under the Baseball Moon, Ritter

Nightjohn, Paulsen

Not every book contains good sentence fluency. As we were selecting mentor texts to recommend in this chapter, we rejected many more than we accepted. We think you will be pleased with the final cut, though. Together, the books showcase a wide range of ways writers make their writing fluent. Whether their sentences are long or short, simple or complex, these books are easy on the ear because their authors combine an equal dose of elegance with the music of fluency for the reader.

Key Quality: Crafting Well-Built Sentences

Owl Moon

Jane Yolen
John Schoenherr, illustrator
Philomel Books, 1987

FOCUS LESSON: Page 105 In this acclaimed narrative, Yolen evokes the darkness and silence of the night, as a young girl and her father venture outside in search of the great horned owl. Here's a sample: "We went into the woods. The shadows were the blackest things I had ever seen. They stained the white snow. My mouth felt furry, for the scarf over it was wet and warm." Writing the book from the girl's perspective was a wise decision. Yolen doesn't just tell a story; she puts us in the story. We are with the girl every step of the way, experiencing her fear, anticipation, and ultimate delight when she spots the bird she's so patiently been seeking. We chose to exclude Caldecott Medal winners from this bibliography, believing that most readers would already be familiar with them. But we made an exception for *Owl Moon*, one of the most fluent picture books of all time.

Old Turtle and the Broken Truth

Douglas Wood
Jon J. Muth, illustrator
Scholastic, 2003

In 1992, *Old Turtle* changed the lives of readers of all ages with its message of peace. In his equally moving follow-up, author Douglas Wood explores the human spirit and its power to unify. His fable is set in a lovely land where "every stone is a teacher and every breeze a language, where every lake is a mirror and every tree a ladder to the stars...." That all changes, though, when a shiny "truth" falls from the sky—a destructive truth that seduces all people of the land, except for one little girl. With life as she knows it disintegrating before her eyes, the little girl seeks the wisdom of Old Turtle, who sees the people's truth not as a whole truth, but as a broken one. The truth can only be mended when we believe "that every person, every being, is important, and that the world was made for each of us." A beautiful story told by a master wordsmith.

The Jade Dragon
Carolyn Marsden and
Virginia Shin-Mui Loh
Candlewick, 2006

Ginny is thrilled when a new girl, Stephanie, joins her class. Ginny, who is Chinese American, has been dying for a friend who is also of Asian heritage, and Stephanie, who was adopted from China by her white parents, seems a likely prospect. The two girls eventually become friends, but their self-concepts are based in very different perspectives. This story explores the complicated emotions and nuances of self-concept that young people experience when they are adopted into and/or belong to a minority culture in their community. Marsden and Loh's thoughtful perspective on this important topic is enhanced by a full range of beautifully constructed sentences. Their book would be interesting to pair with the graphic novel *American Born Chinese* by Gene Luen Yang to compare the different ways sentences are used in each text.

Inkheart
Cornelia Funke
Scholastic, 2003

Funke is a master writer at the sentence level, making sure every word counts. Her fantasy stories draw readers in with more than good story lines; she's great at using phrasing and sentence construction to bring that story to life. In this book, already a modern-day classic, Meggie Folchart and her father Mortimer (Mo) love to read, but no matter how much Meggie begs, her father will not read aloud to her. Meggie discovers that if he reads aloud, characters literally spring from the pages only to be replaced in the book by real people from Mo's life. This power led to the loss of Meggie's mother years earlier into a book and to the escape of the arch villain, Capricorn, into the real world. This book is a gift to readers who love a good book and a well-written story.

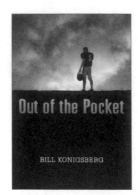

Out of the Pocket

Bill Konigsberg
Dutton, 2008

Bobby Framingham has everything going for him. He is the star quarterback on a football team that should go all the way to the state championship. He has the inside track on a full athletic scholarship to a top university, and he is dating the most intelligent, funny, and beautiful girl at school. Bobby has a secret, however, one that he has been struggling with for some time. He knows that he is gay, and even though he feels like a hypocrite when he ignores homophobic locker room talk, he isn't sure revealing his sexuality would be anything short of disastrous for the team and to his life goals. Professional sportswriter Bill Konigsberg has artfully crafted a story that is compelling for every reader, regardless of his or her sexual or gender identity. From simple statements to complex passages of dialogue, the sentences are a standout in this piece. (Mature Themes)

Hippie Chick

Joseph Monninger
Front Street, 2008

Fifteen-year-old Lolly Emmerson is an expert sailor, so when she takes her sailboat, the *Mugwump*, out to sea on the Florida coast two hours before sunset, it doesn't seem like a dangerous voyage. She could never have predicted that her boat would collide with an underwater snag and roll over or that she would be knocked unconscious. The most unpredictable event, however, was being saved my manatees. Number One, as Lolly calls him, tows her to the safety of an Everglades hot springs, where she recovers from nearly fatal hypothermia and is later discovered and rescued. As Lolly narrates her story, all events are explained from her own calm, introspective, philosophical point of view. The sentences are solid, steady, and contribute to the book's voice. Written as a survival story with ecological overtones, the intentional use of sentences is worth noting in this text.

Key Quality: Varying Sentence Types

Morning on the Lake

Jan Bourdeau Waboose
Karen Reczuch, illustrator
Kids Can Press, 1998

Morning on the Lake is a deceptively simple story. One early morning, a boy and his grandfather go canoeing on a tranquil lake. As the sun rises higher, they climb a rocky cliff for an aerial view of the wilderness below. Finally, as night falls, they venture into the woods in search of natural wonders. The bond that the boy and his grandfather share is undeniably strong—and the lesson the boy learns, to respect nature and all it gives us, is compelling. But what makes this book extraordinary is not what Waboose says, but *how* she says it. Her sentence patterns are remarkably varied, creating a cadence that is pure music to the ear. Take this passage, for example: "Grandfather stops the canoe in the center of the lake. He does not speak. This is his special place. Morning is his favorite time, and so it is mine." Share this book as a model of magnificent craftsmanship.

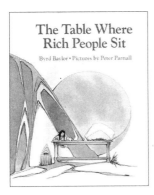

The Table Where Rich People Sit

Byrd Baylor
Peter Parnall, illustrator
Atheneum Books, 1994

In this age of high-priced electronics, celebrity worship, and name-brand clothes, it isn't always easy helping middle school students keep their priorities straight. Telling them how lucky they are to have food on the table and a roof over their head usually falls on deaf ears—they'd rather have new jeans. So we need to be more creative by sharing books with them that speak to the truly important things in life—books like *The Table Where Rich People Sit,* the story of a girl who is discouraged by her family's lack of wealth until her parents calculate the value of watching a sunset, feeling the wind, smelling the rain, and having one another to love. Baylor's sentences move like a force of nature, in fact. Each one is a little different from the next. All of them flow as gently and gracefully as a mountain stream, carrying a message all young people need to hear.

Shiloh

Phyllis Reynolds Naylor
Atheneum, 1991

While hunting in the hills above Friendly, West Virginia, 11-year-old Marty Preston finds a young beagle, a victim of horrible abuse. Shiloh, as Marty calls him, turns out to be the property of one Judd Travers, a known ne'er-do-well. Marty knows that keeping the dog would be stealing, but returning him would be sentencing him to a life of misery. What follows is a moral dilemma—keep the dog and protect him from a life of cruelty or return him as the law dictates. This Newbery Medal–winner has a tight story told in immaculate prose. Every sentence has been skillfully crafted. On any given page you'll find examples of different sentence types woven together to make the story flow off the page and into your heart.

Warrior Angel

Robert Lipsyte
HarperCollins, 2003

Sonny Bear is the heavyweight boxing champion of the world, and although everyone, from movie stars to the Nike Corporation, pretends to love him, it's hard for him to tell who his real friends are. His motivation for boxing is already waning at 20 years of age, and the primary motivation of his entourage seems to be cashing in as quickly as possible on Sonny's celebrity, regardless of what is best for him. When a message comes to his secret e-mail address from the "Warrior Angel," telling Sonny he is coming on a mission from the Creator to save Sonny, Sonny is the only one who takes it seriously. The story is told in alternating voices. Lipsyte, a seasoned pro at bringing out the voice in every character, steps into the sentence fluency ring in this book, big-time.

Tasting the Sky

Ibtisam Barakat
Farrar, Straus and Giroux, 2007

"When a war ends, it does not go away. It hides inside us." So explains Ibtisam Barakat's mother in 1981, at the end of this autobiographical account of a Palestinian girl that spans 14 years, beginning with the Six-Day War in 1967. Ibtisam relates the fear and vulnerability of living under the rule of foreign power, using beautifully written prose that showcases the best of what sentences are meant to do—make the ideas resonate. The narrator is only three-and-a-half years old when the war begins. Her life takes a dramatic turn as she experiences the everyday threat of detainment, interrogation, or the possibility of imprisonment or worse for herself, her family, and friends. Simple sentences with "just the facts" interspersed with complex sentences that chronicle the narrator's memories help make this book so effective.

Does My Head Look Big in This?
Randa Abdel-Fattah
Scholastic, 2005

FOCUS LESSON: Page 107 When Amal Mohamed Nasrullah Abdel-Hakim has a cathartic moment while walking on the treadmill and watching TV, it comes from an unlikely source: the character Rachel from the sitcom "Friends." Amal decides that she will express her devotion to her Islamic heritage and begin wearing the hijab, the traditional head covering of Islamic women. Never mind that her Palestinian-born parents have lived in Australia for fifty-two years and that Amal was raised in a "trendy suburb" of Melbourne. She decides, "I want to prove to myself that I am strong enough to wear a badge of my faith." She has no idea what she is about to encounter—at school, at the mall, with friends, anywhere. Abdel-Fattah writes with a quick tempo, using varied sentence patterns to reveal moments of cruelty, hilarity, and romance.

Key Quality: Capturing Smooth and Rhythmic Flow

Sitti's Secrets
Naomi Shihab Nye
Nancy Carpenter, illustrator
Simon & Schuster, 1994

Mona lives in the United States. Her grandmother, her "Sitti," lives in Palestine. Despite the "many miles of land and water" that separate them, despite the fact that they don't speak the same language, they are as close as two people can be. One day, Mona visits Sitti to learn what life is like in her small village. She enjoys the simple pleasures of baking bread in Sitti's old oven, drinking lemonade made from the fruit of Sitti's trees, and brushing Sitti's long hair that she typically keeps hidden under a scarf. Life is good. When the time comes to leave, Mona is sad, but confident that mere geography cannot destroy the bond she shares with Sitti. Nye is a writer's writer. She crafts and combines sentences in the same way Sitti prepares meals and stitches fabric—with utmost attention to detail. There is much for your students to learn from her here.

Jazz ABZ: An A to Z Collection of Jazz Portraits

Wynton Marsalis
Paul Rogers, illustrator
Candlewick Press, 2005

Dizzie Gillespie, Fats Waller, and Billie Holiday—just mentioning their names conjures up the sounds of trumpets, pianos, and magnificent voices. This dazzling catalogue brings to life those and 23 other jazz greats through poetry. Marsalis ingeniously writes about each musician in a specific poetic form—common ones (such as ode, sonnet, and limerick) and more obscure ones (such as tanka, rondeau, and skeltonic verse). And his poems are electrifying. They pounce and glide like jazz itself. This format not only introduces students to important figures in musical history, but also gives them options to choose from when they sit down to write. Have your students choose their own nonfiction topic, organize details about it alphabetically, and create poems. You'll be singing their praises.

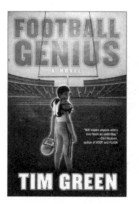

Football Genius

Tim Green
HarperCollins, 2007

FOCUS LESSON: Page 109 Troy White has the ability to predict the offense's next play in any football game, but when he attempts to help the defensive coach of his favorite team, the Atlanta Falcons, Troy causes two things to happen: (1) he is removed from the playing field, twice, and (2) his single mother is fired from her new job in public relations with the Falcons. Packed with interesting characters, all of whom who love football for different reasons, this piece reads so smoothly it takes a second look to appreciate the specific elements that contribute to this overall effect. Green is more than a former star defensive end for the Atlanta Falcons. He's a natural storyteller, using rhythmic and graceful sentences from beginning to end.

A Single Shard

Linda Sue Park
Yearling, 2003

Tree Ear is an orphan living in the remote village of Ch'ul'po, famous for its pottery, in twelfth-century Korea. Although Tree Ear is dying to become a potter and does everything he can think of to win the approval of Min, the old potter, Min refuses to take on any apprentice other than his own son, a tradition that is unfamiliar to Tree Ear. This Newbery Medal–winner reads like silk. It passes the test for ease of reading aloud: "Tree-Ear could hardly breathe on his walk home. Min's words rang in his ears, over and over: *orphaned one . . . father to son . . . not my son.* He realized now what he had never thought to notice before: All the other apprentices were indeed sons of the potters."

Life, Love, and the Pursuit of Free Throws

Janette Rallison
Walker, 2004

High school freshmen Josie and Cami are best friends. They hang out together, do homework together, play basketball together and confide in each other their innermost desires. For example, Josie is madly in love with Ethan Lancaster, and Cami dreams of running plays with retired WNBA star Rebecca Lobo when she does a halftime program for Sanchez High. The problem is that Josie is a shoo-in for MVP and the honor of playing with Rebecca Lobo, and Cami catches Ethan Lancaster's attention easily. Each friend is on track to realize the other friend's dream. How do they handle that? Carefully, very carefully. Rallison is skilled at keeping the action moving with natural dialogue that sounds like each character. The result is an easy-on-the-ear story.

The Face on the Milk Carton

Caroline B. Cooney
Random House, 1990

Janie Johnson is about as normal as a high school sophomore can be. Her parents have agreed that she is old enough to learn how to drive but not old enough to date. She has lots of friends, pretty good grades, and hates her name, which is just too plain. Her life is comfortably uneventful until she thinks she recognizes a 10-year-old picture of herself on the back of a milk carton advertising for a missing child. Does she really remember "that dress . . . how the collar itched. . . . [how] the wind blew through it. . . "? Janie's mind races as memories come forward, setting her on an investigation of her own past. What Janie finds out is told through smooth, flowing prose delivered ingeniously by Cooney. (Mature Themes)

Key Quality: Breaking the "Rules" to Create Fluency

Show Way

Jacqueline Woodson
Hudson Talbott, illustrator
G. P. Putnam's Sons, 2005

We admire so many things about Woodson: her authentic voice, her carefully chosen words, her original ideas that cut straight to the heart. But mostly we admire her willingness to embrace issues that few writers are willing to, such as substance abuse, parental incarceration, racism, and homophobia. These issues, we know, aren't fit for every classroom. But for children who are touched by them, Woodson's books are a balm. *Show Way* is, perhaps, her most personal book. It is the story of a tradition that has been passed down by the women in her family, from slavery to the Civil Rights Movement, as a way to remember the past and ensure a better life for future generations. Like all of Woodson's books, *Show Way* does not preach. It is an honest story, written in a lyrical vernacular voice, inspired by a legacy of love.

Once Upon a Cool Motorcycle Dude

Kevin O'Malley, author and illustrator
Carol Heyer, illustrator
Scott Goto, illustrator
Walker & Company, 2005

By the time we make it to middle school, most of us are brainwashed to believe that girls are made of "everything nice" and boys are made of, well, "puppy dog tails." *Once Upon a Cool Motorcycle Dude* challenges that dichotomy. In it, a typical girl and typical boy make up a fairy tale. The girl starts, introducing us to Princess Tenderheart, whose beloved ponies are being snatched away by a horrible giant, one by one. The boy continues the tale, saving the day not with a handsome prince, but with "a cool muscle dude." The kids are horrified by one another's ideas, until they join forces to come up with a mutually satisfying ending. The mix of illustration styles, typeface styles, running text, and speech bubbles makes this book a treat for the senses. Let student pairs read it aloud together to see and hear O'Malley's superb sentence fluency. They'll have a blast.

When the Circus Came to Town

Polly Horvath
Farrar, Straus and Giroux, 1998

Springfield is a boring town to begin with, and Ivy's parents are way too predictable, but when Ivy is bedridden with pneumonia, boredom hits an all-time high. And then the Halibuts moved in next door. If nine rooms of red and yellow furniture delivered before their arrival don't give it away, the parade of circus performers into Springfield makes it irrefutable: The circus has come to town. A strong man, a fortune teller, a snake charmer, and the Flying Gambinis simply want to call Springfield home, maybe even contribute to the community bake sale. When the citizens treat the newcomers poorly, however, Ivy will get down to business, taming a gang and facing prejudice head-on. Horvath delivers a fun read peppered with dialogue, rhetorical questions, and a few fragments here and there to make the book energetic and natural-sounding.

The Music of Dolphins

Karen Hesse, author
Scholastic, 1996

FOCUS LESSON: Page 112

When four-year-old Mila's parents are killed in a plane crash at sea, she is rescued by dolphins, which raise her in the shallow waters off the Florida coast. She is "saved" by the Coast Guard years later and delivered to scientific researchers studying feral children. Life imprisoned in the laboratory is miserable for Mila, however, and as her outlook steadily deteriorates, so does the experiment. Mila tells her own story, recorded on a computer each day for the scientists' data collection. As the story begins, she uses incomplete sentences and simple words, but as Mila's command of English improves, so does the complexity of her syntax and the sophistication of her ideas. The story's pivotal message about the ethics of scientific research and the nature of humanity is enhanced by the creative and effective sentence structure throughout.

Under the Baseball Moon

John H. Ritter
Penguin, 2006

Andy Ramos describes himself as "a little star-crossed and over the moon." Not only has Andy formed a fusion band (jazz, rock, and hip-hop, with a Latino flare), but there is also a fusion between his trumpet playing and Gloria Martinez's softball pitching. San Diego's Ocean Beach is the perfect setting for this magical, mythical tale that includes Max Lucero, a mysterious stranger who may not be a stranger after all. This story is told with unusual sentence flair. It's rich with phrasing that is as interesting as the story itself. Spanish language and Latino culture give the story character and humorous wordplay, as in "OB Juan Quixote's seafood taco bar and grill." John Ritter is a master at crafting baseball stories into mesmerizing fairy tales—no small feat.

Nightjohn
Gary Paulsen
Laurel Leaf, 1995

This story is told through the eyes of Sarny, a twelve-year-old slave girl living on a Plantation in the deep South just before the Civil War. Nightjohn, a recently purchased slave, shares a secret with her: He can read. Although it holds unspeakable punishment if they are caught, Sarny attends Nightjohn's underground school and learns to read. He tells Sarny, "To know things, for us to know things, is bad for them. We get to wanting and when we get to wanting it's bad for them. They thinks we want what they got. . . . That's why they don't want us reading." Paulsen's intentional use of sentence fragments and nonstandard syntax suggest a protagonist who has only recently become literate. The resulting voice feels authentic, like that of a young girl whose hatred and hope have found an outlet on the page. (Mature Themes)

Focus Lesson 1: Crafting Well-Built Sentences

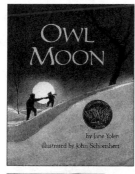

PICTURE BOOK

Owl Moon
Jane Yolen

Think About the Writer's Work:

- Do the sentences begin in different ways?

- Are the sentences different lengths?

- Are the sentences built with sturdy construction?

- Did she use transitions (*but, and, so*) to connect parts of sentences?

Lesson Focus:

Go to any place in this narrative about a young girl and her father who go out into the woods "owling," and you'll be drawn in by elegant and beautiful sentences that flow across the page. In this lesson, students study this exquisitely written book for ideas on making their writing equally strong in sentence fluency.

Materials:

- a copy of *Owl Moon*

- projection and copies of the Think About the Writer's Work questions above

- projections of selected illustrations and passages

- paper, pens, pencils

What to Do:

1. Explain to students that expert writers think a lot about how sentences are individually constructed and how they are joined together to create a fluent piece of writing. Project and discuss the Think About the Writer's Work questions and give students a copy to refer to during the lesson.

2. Read *Owl Moon* to students from beginning to end without stopping. If possible, project the pages using a document camera so students can see the text and pictures clearly. Otherwise, be sure the book is facing the class as you read. When you're finished, ask students if they heard sentence fluency and how they recognized it.

3. Ask students to make a chart with five columns and five rows.

Sentence:	Number of words in the sentence:	First two words:	Type of sentence:	Interesting to note...
1.				
2.				
3.				
4.				
5.				

4. As a class, fill in information about sentences on page 1. In the second column, write down the number of words in each sentence; in the third column, the first two words in each; in the fourth column, the type of each sentence (simple, compound, complex, compound–complex); and in the fifth column, anything you find interesting about each sentence. Discuss how your findings relate to the book's sentence fluency.

Sentence:	Number of words in the sentence:	First two words:	Type of sentence:	Interesting to note...
1.	16	It was	complex	Identifies main characters and time of day
2.	4	There was	simple	Much shorter than first sentence
3.	7	The trees	simple	Nice use of a simile
4.	11	And the	compound	Begins with "And"
5.	15	Somewhere behind	complex	Repetition of the word "sad" for emphasis

5. Put students into groups of three or four and ask them to chart another page from the book. The length of their chart will depend on the number of sentences on the page they select. Remind them to use the Think About the Writer's Work questions for clues about what constitutes sentence fluency. Once they've finished, let groups share their results and any interesting things they noticed about the sentences on their selected page.

6. Ask students to think of an activity or event that was very special to them and write a fluent paragraph about it, using the same structures and lengths as the sentences on the page they charted.

7. When they've finished, invite a few students to read their pieces and discuss whether it was easy or difficult to replicate Yolen's style and why.

Lesson Extension:

Ask students to chart a passage of nonfiction text and compare the results to those from *Owl Moon*. Specifically, invite students to explore magazines, newspapers, and other readily available nonfiction resources to find a particularly fluent passage. Once they agree upon a passage, chart it out as a class as you did for *Owl Moon*, discuss any differences between sentence structure and length in fiction and nonfiction, and hang the chart for students to refer to as they write.

Focus Lesson 2: Varying Sentence Types

YOUNG ADULT NOVEL

Does My Head Look Big in This?
Randa Abdel-Fattah

Think About the Writer's Work:

• Did the writer include different kinds of sentences?

• Are some of her sentences complex?

• Are some of her sentences simple?

• Did she intermingle sentence types, one to the next?

Lesson Focus:

Amal, an Australian-Palestinian girl living in a suburb of Melbourne, makes a decision that dramatically affects her life—to wear the hijab, the Muslim headscarf. Why she makes this decision and how she handles the harassment that results from it is revealed fluently in Amal's ongoing internal dialogue and her interactions with friends, family members, and narrow-minded classmates. In this lesson, students choose an issue that's important to them, take a position on that issue, and explain that position in a short written dialogue using sentences of different lengths to make the writing fluent.

Materials:

• a copy of *Does My Head Look Big in This?*

• projection and copies of the Think About the Writer's Work questions above

• paper, pens, pencils

• projection of the following passage from Chapter 8:

> "Everybody's scared of what they don't know, Amal."
>
> I tilt my head back and roll my eyes at my mom. She gives me an exasperated look in return.
>
> "You still have a lot to learn, darling," she says.
>
> "Oh *puh-lease* don't give me that line, Mom!" She smiles and hugs me even tighter....
>
> "...As far as I'm concerned, if you want to think you're going to heaven because you believe guys should go to school and get to do what they want but girls have to stay home till they're ready to be married, then go fly a kite. I don't care why you don't know any better. When you have a kid who knows more about your religion than you do and is smart enough to be anything she wants, then in my book you lose your right to excuses."

What to Do:

1. Summarize the plot of *Does My Head Look Big in This?* Explain that the main character, Amal, makes an important decision based on her Muslim heritage and a belief that reason can triumph over prejudice.

2. Read aloud the passage and ask students to explain what it tells them about Amal. Show students the Think About the Writer's Work questions and discuss them. Reread the passage and ask students to note the different types of sentences that Abdel-Fattah uses.

3. Make a chart with four headings: simple sentence, compound sentence, complex sentences, and compound/complex sentence.

Simple	Compound	Complex	Compound/Complex

4. Number the sentences in the passage 1–9. Ask students to tell you which type of sentence each is and put the number of the sentence under the correct heading. Before doing this activity, review the definitions of sentence types.

Simple	A sentence made up of one independent clause that may contain a direct object or prepositional phrase
Compound	A sentence made up of two or more independent clauses that are joined by a conjunction such as *and*, *but*, or *or*
Complex	A sentence made up of an independent clause and at least one dependent clause
Compound-Complex	A sentence made up of two or more independent clauses and at least one dependent clause

Remind students that a clause is a sentence part that contains a subject and verb; an independent clause can stand alone as a grammatically correct sentence; a dependent clause cannot stand alone.

Simple	Compound	Complex	Compound/Complex
1, 3, 4, 5, 8	2, 6	9	7

5. Discuss what Abdel-Fattah does to create fluency. Students might note that she uses techniques in addition to varying the sentences by adding dialogue, passionate voice, and natural-sounding phrasing. Write their ideas on the whiteboard.

6. Ask students how they would feel if they were told to wear an article of clothing or a piece of jewelry that represented something personal about them, such as their religion, gender, or age.

7. Ask students to pick something they want to wear, something that represents a belief or an interest, and describe it. Then ask them to imagine that their peers make fun of them for wearing it.

8. Have students write the internal and external dialogue the students might have as they express their feelings about their choice of what to wear and why it matters to them. Ask them to try and use at least one of each sentence type in their dialogue.

9. Invite volunteers to share their writing with the class and discuss how external dialogue and internal dialogue helped to make the writing fluent. Discuss their use of different sentence types and which were the easiest and which were the most difficult to work into the text. Use the Think About the Writer's Work questions to guide the conversation.

Lesson Extension:

Ask students if feeling strongly about the issue helped them write more fluently. From there, discuss the relationship between sentence fluency and voice.

Next, have students browse the library for other books that address controversial topics, such as *Fahrenheit 451, The Giver, A Day No Pigs Would Die, The Catcher in the Rye,* and *I Know Why the Caged Bird Sings.* Tell them to choose one book and look for fluent passages that use different types of sentences in which two or more characters discuss the topic and the main character engages in an internal dialogue.

Focus Lesson 3: Capturing Smooth and Rhythmic Flow

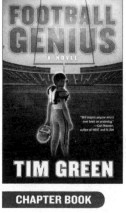

Football Genius
Tim Green

Think About the Writer's Work:

- Is the book easy to read aloud?

- Do his sentences flow easily from one to the next?

- Does he use phrases that sound smooth?

- Do the sentences have a pleasing tempo?

Lesson Focus:

In this fast-paced story, twelve-year-old Troy White struggles to get playing time on his school football team. A teammate pushes Troy to seek help from a local pro football hero, who eventually teaches Troy all the right moves to take his rightful place leading the team. But even more important, he helps Troy sort through his feelings about being abandoned by his father. Every reader who's ever been an underdog will appreciate Green's inspiration and wisdom. In this lesson, students examine a passage from *Football Genius* for sentence fluency, noting the techniques Green uses to create a smooth flow from beginning to end.

Materials:

- a copy of *Football Genius*
- projection and copies of the Think About the Writer's Work questions above
- projection of the following passage from Chapter 45:

> When the ball was snapped, Seth made a beeline for the strong side. Troy turned his shoulders and leaned, the same as Seth did as he slipped through a gap in the line. Then Troy dropped his hips and threw his arms around the air in front of him, just as Seth did the same to the runner, lifting him off his feet and driving him back to the turf. The crowd went wild. Intoxicated by the deafening thunder of applause, Troy leaped forward and ran halfway out onto the field as Seth came running off with a swarm of teammates around him. Seth wrapped his arms around Troy and lifted him in a bear hug, bounding off the field and mussing his hair and roaring all at the same time.
>
> "You did it, buddy! You did it!" Seth screamed, setting Troy down beside his mom and ignoring the jostling smacks his teammates put on his shoulder pads and back.

What to Do:

1. Review with students the Think About the Writer's Work questions and discuss different ways authors make their writing flow smoothly and rhythmically. Write their ideas on the whiteboard for them to refer to during the lesson, embellishing them as you see fit. Suggestions might include:

   - creating sentences of different lengths
   - varying types of sentences—simple, compound, complex, compound-complex
   - using dialogue
   - using alliteration
   - using transition words and sequence words
   - ending sentences on a solid, one-syllable note
   - using punctuation to create phrases and clauses
   - beginning sentences differently

2. Project the passage and ask students to follow along as you read it aloud, listening carefully for how it sounds, not only for what it says.

3. Read the passage again and, this time, ask students to note where the author used techniques listed on the whiteboard to make the writing smooth.

4. When you finish reading, have students call out what they noticed. They might say:

   • sentence one has an adverbial clause set off with a comma

   • sentence two is complex

   • the use of *then* as a sequence word in sentence three

   • the sentences end with words of single syllables

   • sentence 3 is long; sentence 4 is short

   • use of dialogue in the second paragraph

   • alliteration in second paragraph: "Seth screamed, setting"

5. Put students into pairs and have them look for more examples of fluent writing in other books. When a pair has found an example of fluent writing, ask them next to find an example of writing that is not fluent. Remind them to use their Think About the Writer's Work questions to guide their decisions.

6. Share the fluent examples with the class and discuss the techniques the writers use. From there, share pieces that were not as strong in this trait and discuss ways to revise them.

7. Ask students to revise the less fluent pieces using the techniques they learned about in this lesson. Invite volunteers to read aloud the original pieces and revised pieces so the class can hear the differences in fluency.

Lesson Extension:

Encourage students to continue finding examples of fluent writing in texts they read and hear every day. Ask them to write down particularly interesting and fluent passages, record themselves reading the passages, and upload their recordings to the school's Web site so their classmates can listen to fluent writing on their own.

Focus Lesson

Focus Lesson 4: Breaking the "Rules" to Create Fluency

CHAPTER BOOK

The Music of Dolphins
Karen Hesse

Think About the Writer's Work:

- Do the fragments add style?

- Do sentences begin informally to make them conversational?

- Does she make dialogue sound real?

- Did she use one-word sentences to add emphasis?

Lesson Focus:

In this critically acclaimed novel that explores what it means to be human, four-year-old Mila survives a plane crash and lives with dolphins for almost ten years. After she's "rescued" by the Coast Guard and returned home safely, scientists study her to learn how she survived in the wild for so long. Mila, however, yearns to return to the sea. In this lesson, students examine various passages from the book for ways in which Hesse takes risks with the sentence structure, patterns, and flow. From there, they write a Web review of *The Music of Dolphins*, focusing on its sentence fluency.

Materials:

- a copy of *The Music of Dolphins*

- projection and copies of the Think About the Writer's Work questions above

- projections of the following passages:

  - Newspaper article after the prologue

  - One page: Chapter 3

  - One page: Chapter 16

  - Mila's story: Chapter 26

  - One page: Chapter 37

  - One page: Chapter 47

  - One page: Chapter 55

  - Chapter 62

What to Do:

1. Explain to students the story line of *The Music of Dolphins* and share that Hesse uses sentence structure and patterns to deepen the meaning and the message of the book.

2. Share the Think About the Writer's Work questions and point out that Hesse deliberately breaks the rules so that her sentences create a specific, fluent sound.

3. Explain to students that you are going to show them a progression of passages from the book. You will begin with the opening pages and end with the final pages. Show the opening pages that contain the newspaper article documenting Mila's discovery and extraordinary life. Discuss what students notice about the sentences: varied, well-constructed, easy-to-read aloud, rich in dialogue, and so on.

4. Show Chapter 3. Discuss why Hesse may have changed the sentences' sound and their structure, progressing from simple to compound and complex as Mila learns English and tells her story.

5. Continue showing subsequent passages from the book, noting that the sentences become more complex and interesting as Mila gains more control over English and learns to articulate more-complex thoughts. Remind students to consult their Think About the Writer's Work questions to help them notice how the writer breaks rules with sentences to enhance the idea.

6. After sharing the first paragraph of Chapter 26, ask students why this passage not only sounds different but is written differently from the earlier passages you shared. Students may respond by saying that this is where Mila shares what she knows of her dolphin world, so the language Hesse uses is passionate and expressive.

7. Read the rest of the passages and ask students about changes in language they notice between each one. Students may note that while the writing is sophisticated and complex at the beginning of the book, it becomes rawer and simpler as Mila yearns to return to the sea.

8. Read the last chapter aloud and ask students to discuss its sentences.

9. Discuss how the author structured sentences and broke rules to make the idea of the story clear and fluent. Ask students to write a one-page summary of the book for a movie producer to review as he or she considers turning the book into a film. Focus on Hesse's techniques for crafting fluent sentences and on how breaking the rules might make the movie interesting to viewers.

Lesson Extension:

Put students into pairs and ask them to select a short chapter from *The Music of Dolphins* to read aloud as a choral reading. Once partners have had ample time to practice, have them perform the readings for the class, beginning with the earliest chapter and ending with the last one. As an extra fluency challenge, ask a few willing students to plan and read aloud Mila's thoughts from Chapter 26 as well as those at the end of the book. Contrast the sound of these sentences with those performed in the earlier choral readings. Discuss the different ways passages sound, based on their sentence structures.

Focus Lesson

CHAPTER 6

Conventions

off the mark.com — by Mark Parisi

THOSE ARE THE RETIRED JERSEYS OF SPELLING BEE CHAMPS...

Onomatopoeia all...ion

CREATIVE ATTEMPTS TO GET THE SAME BUZZ AS THE SPORTS PROGRAM

© Mark Parisi

et's face it, going to a spelling bee will never have the same appeal as going to the Friday night football game. But spelling is important and deserves a starting position on the conventions team, along with all the others—capitalization, punctuation, paragraphing, and grammar and usage— because this is how the writer makes text easy to read. And in the writing game, that's a big part of how readers decide if they win or lose.

Conventions are the editing standards we apply to a piece of writing to make it mechanically correct and, therefore, a simple task to read. Each convention has its own set of rules—rules a copy editor follows to prepare text for publication. Rules that must be taught to middle school students so they can apply them with accuracy and consistency to their writing.

We edit for conventions because we care about our reader. Whether our reader is a teacher, a peer, or the general public, we want him or her to be able to follow our writing effortlessly and become immersed in our ideas, which can only happen if he or she is not bogged down by unintentional errors. There are standard conventions to which we must adhere, unless we depart from them for a clear purpose. To show strength in conventions, the writer must skillfully and confidently apply these key qualities:

* **Checking Spelling**
  The writer spells sight words, high-frequency words, and less familiar words correctly. When he or she spells less familiar words incorrectly, those words are phonetically correct. Overall, the piece reveals control in spelling.

* **Punctuating Effectively and Paragraphing Accurately**
  The writer handles basic punctuation skillfully. He or she understands how to use periods, commas, question marks, and exclamation points to enhance clarity and meaning. Paragraphs are indented in the right places. The piece is ready for a general audience.

* **Capitalizing Correctly**
  The writer uses capital letters consistently and accurately. A deep understanding of how to capitalize dialogue, abbreviations, proper names, and titles is evident.

* **Applying Grammar and Usage**
  The writer forms grammatically correct phrases and sentences. He or she shows care in applying the rules of standard English. The writer may break from those rules for stylistic reasons, but otherwise abides by them.

In our experience, middle school teachers will try every trick imaginable to make their students realize the importance of applying conventions accurately in their writing. Most students, though, don't pay attention; they view editing as boring, irrelevant, or both. But teachers have to keep trying, because their students' readers just won't put up with lots of errors—no matter how inspired the piece may be in the other traits.

Of course, the books we selected for this chapter contain correct conventions. After all, it's reasonable to expect that any published book has been edited for accuracy. So we picked these books because they show something interesting about conventions—something that your students might want to apply in their own work.

Mentor Texts in This Chapter

Checking Spelling
Mom and Dad Are Palindromes, Shulman

Eight Ate: A Feast of Homonym Riddles, Terban

Bloomability, Creech

The City of Ember, DuPrau

Down the Yukon, Hobbs

My Name Is Seepeetza, Sterling

Punctuating Effectively and Paragraphing Accurately
Twenty-Odd Ducks: Why, Every Punctuation Mark Counts! Truss

Greedy Apostrophe: A Cautionary Tale, Carr

Many Thousand Gone, Hamilton

Strange Happenings, Avi

Love Me, Love My Broccoli, Peters

Bury My Heart at Wounded Knee, Brown

Capitalizing Correctly
Code Blue: Calling All Capitals! Hall

Explorer, Matthews

Black Star, Bright Dawn, O'Dell

Dump Trucks and Dogsleds: I'm on My Way, Mom! Winkler and Oliver

Soldier's Heart, Paulsen

Code Talker, Bruchac

Applying Grammar and Usage
Word Fun Series:

If You Were an Adjective, Dahl

If You Were an Adverb, Dahl

If You Were an Antonym, Loewen

If You Were a Conjunction, Loewen

If You Were a Noun, Dahl

If You Were a Preposition, Loewen

If You Were a Synonym, Dahl

If You Were a Verb, Dahl

Matilda, Dahl

Slam! Myers

I Am a Star: Child of the Holocaust, Auerbacher

Men on the Moon, Ortiz

Share the high-energy picture books to begin conversations about each convention. Who can resist *Greedy Apostrophe*? Or *Twenty-Odd Ducks: Why, Every Punctuation Mark Counts!*? Or *Eight Ate: A Feast of Homonym Riddles*? Books like these will not only heighten your students' awareness of spelling, capitalization, punctuation, paragraphing, and grammar and usage, they'll change students' attitude about editing and help them see how important it is.

The chapter books and young adult novels listed here are models of what each convention looks like when it's under control. Students need to see strong conventions in action to consider possibilities for their own writing. Strong conventions follow the rules of standard English, guiding the reader through the text with familiar road signs. Sometimes they accomplish even more, however. They can be used cleverly to get the reader's attention, for example, capitalizing whole words to show emphasis, leaving out punctuation to create a sense of breathlessness, creating new words to match new thinking, or writing dialogue in nonstandard English to bring a character to life. Using conventions for stylistic reasons can make the writing more engaging and has the bonus effect of making the writing more fun for both reader AND writer.

In your classroom, you will find many other books that apply conventions correctly and even creatively. As you run across them, be sure to flag passages to share with students. By shining a light on how the authors of those books handle conventions, your students will more likely want to "get it right" in their own work. We hope the books in this chapter give you a good start.

Key Quality: Checking Spelling

Mom and Dad Are Palindromes
Mark Shulman
Adam McCauley, illustrator
Chronicle Books, 2006

Bob's got a problem. He is surrounded by palindromes—words, phrases, and sentences that are spelled exactly the same way forward and backward—including his "kayak," his "race car," his dog, "Otto," and his teacher, "Miss Sim." Real panic sets in when he goes to "Mom" and "Dad" for help and realizes that they, too, are palindromes! But when Bob learns that synonyms, such as "Mother" and "Father," exist for those words, he relaxes. Shulman's creative storytelling will grab your students' attention from page one and won't let go until students have discovered all the palindromes in the book, including those the author has cleverly included on bulletin boards, book spines, movie marquees, and other inconspicuous places. The English language is filled with palindromes, more than you and your students might imagine. Building awareness of them has never been this much fun.

Eight Ate: A Feast of Homonym Riddles

Marvin Terban
Giulio Maestro, illustrator
Houghton Mifflin Company, 1982

How many times have your students meant to write "their" and given you "there"... or "wear" and given you "where"... or "you're" and given you "your"? Too many times, we suspect. This book will not only help students spell homonyms correctly, it will also make them guffaw, chuckle, and laugh out loud. Here's the proof: "What is a smelly chicken? A foul fowl." "What is a sailor's bellybutton? A naval navel." "Who is married to Uncle Beetle? Aunt Ant." As corny has these riddles may be, they are a refreshing and effective alternative to traditional spelling lists and Friday quizzes. In addition to *Eight Ate*, Terban has written a whole host of wordplay books, including *In a Pickle: And Other Funny Idioms* and *The Dove Dove: Funny Homograph Riddles*. Bring them all into your classroom to get students looking at language as they never have before.

Bloomability

Sharon Creech
HarperCollins, 1998

By the time Dinnie is twelve years old, she has lived in 12 states and has so few worldly possessions they "fit in one box." When she goes to live with her Aunt Sandy and Uncle Max, she imagines herself in a bubble as her alter ego, Domenica Santolina Doone, flying away to Switzerland to become a student at the international school her aunt and uncle run. Despite her desire for emotional sanctuary, Dinnie finds herself making many friends with other young people from around the world who have come to this beautiful place to explore possibilities, or "bloomabilities" as Dinnie's Japanese friend, Keisuke puts it. Skiing in the Alps, surviving an avalanche, participating in other adventures cause Dinnie to conclude that "anything could happen, anything at all. The bloomabilities were endless." The names of European people and places is one of the many things that makes this book special.

Questions to Ask When Choosing Books

When browsing the bookstore or library for books to use when teaching about conventions, ask yourself:

- Does the book contain a lot of good examples of common spelling, capitalization, punctuation, and/or grammar and usage rules?

- Does the book contain a lot of words that my students typically spell and/or capitalize incorrectly?

- Does it contain a lot of sentence types that my students typically punctuate and/or structure incorrectly?

- Has the author used standard English spelling, capitalization, punctuation, and/or grammar and usage—or has he or she chosen to subvert it for a good reason?

- Has the author used standard English spelling, capitalization, punctuation, and/or grammar and usage not only correctly but also creatively for stylistic reasons—to highlight a point, set a pace, or emphasize a word or phrase, for example?

The City of Ember: The First Book of Ember
Jeanne DuPrau
Random House, 2003

Two hundred forty years after an apocalypse sends survivors to live deep under Earth's surface, the City of Ember remains a fully self-contained world for a community of people who know no other way of life. The creators of the city planned for the residents to return to the surface 200 years after its creation, but the seventh mayor failed to pass on the "Instructions for Egress" before his death. Eventually, those instructions fall into the hands of young Lina and Doon, who find that, despite the fact that Ember's infrastructure and food supply are deteriorating, the city authorities have no intention of an exodus to the surface. Lina and Doon bravely explore the unknown regions of their underground world and escape. Will others follow? Jeanne DuPrau sustains a very palpable feeling of darkness that is never illuminated by anything but an electric light that is beginning to flicker. Unusual proper nouns, such as "Quillium" and "Bilbollio Squares," call for spelling skills that students will be inspired to master.

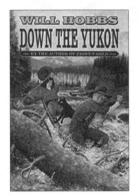

Down the Yukon
Will Hobbs
HarperCollins, 2001

In *Jason's Gold*, brothers Ethan and Jason Hawthorn are among the thousands of fortune seekers who rushed to Canada's Yukon Valley in the late 1800s, when gold was discovered there. In this sequel, sixteen-year-old Jason looks for a way to regain Ethan's sawmill after the title is lost under suspicious circumstances. When a canoe race down the Yukon River is announced, Jason, his girlfriend Jamie, and a canine companion named Burnt Paw enter, with hopes of using the $20,000 first prize to buy back the sawmill. Their trip downriver is fraught with hazards, including dangerous animals and outlaws who would prevent them from achieving a fair victory. Hobbs has the story's details, time, and place in history down pat because of his intensive research and his own experiences in the wilds of the Yukon. His use of indigenous words for places and people in the Yukon Territory add to the book's authenticity.

My Name Is Seepeetza
Shirley Sterling
Groundwood Books, 1992

At her boarding school for indigenous children of British Columbia, Kalamak Indian Residential School, Seepeetza is considered a "status Indian" by law. As such, she is punished for speaking in her native dialect, using her birth name, looking at boys in church, stepping out of line, writing anything about the school in her letters home, or attempting to leave the dorm or recreation room. When she wets the bed, the nuns make her wear the soiled sheets over her head and won't allow her to drink anything after five o'clock. Seepeetza's life at home on the ranch, on the other hand, is idyllic, and even though she despises school and is well aware of the crimes perpetrated on children by clergy there, she remains a devout Catholic. Based on the Sterling's own life in the 1950s, this story is told simply, in the authentic voice of a teenage girl. Place names in English, French, and Salish (the indigenous language of the area) make the language of this book fascinating to study.

Key Quality: Punctuating Effectively and Paragraphing Accurately

Twenty-Odd Ducks: Why, Every Punctuation Mark Counts!
Lynne Truss
Bonnie Timmons, illustrator
G. P. Putnam's Sons, 2008

With *Eats, Shoots & Leaves* and *The Girl's Like Spaghetti*, Truss proved that commas and apostrophes can be a writer's best friends or worst enemies, depending on how they call out to him or her. They can either help the writer say precisely what he or she wants to say—or sweet-talk the writer into saying something he or she doesn't mean at all. In *Twenty-Odd Ducks: Why, Every Punctuation Mark Counts!* Truss takes on a whole flock of punctuation marks—commas, apostrophes, hyphens, parentheses, quotation marks, question marks, exclamation points, colons, periods—with the same cautionary gusto. If a writer says, for example, "The queen: without her, dinner is noisy," she means while the queen's away, the guests will play... loudly. Whereas if the same writer says, "The queen, without her dinner, is noisy," she means a hungry queen is a cranky queen. Without question, your students will get Truss's point. Period.

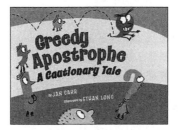

Greedy Apostrophe: A Cautionary Tale
Jan Carr
Ethan Long, illustrator
Holiday House, 2007

Assignment day has arrived for all punctuation marks.
The question marks wonder what their jobs will be. The exclamation points are confident they'll land plumb ones. The commas pause, awaiting a verdict. Finally, the Director of Punctuation begins the proceedings. He assigns an exclamation point to a "danger" sign, a group of quotation marks to a newspaper interview, and three apostrophes to the song title, "Baby, I'm Here, You're Here, So Let's Dance." Everyone's thrilled—except for one apostrophe, Greedy Apostrophe, who is stuck with the

most unglamorous of jobs: creating possessives. So he takes revenge by jumping into signs where he doesn't belong—and confusing the daylights out of anyone who reads those signs. What will it take to stop Greedy Apostrophe and put him in his place? Carr will have your students cheering, chuckling, and champing at the bit to learn the rules of apostrophe use.

Many Thousand Gone: African Americans From Slavery to Freedom
Virginia Hamilton
Leo and Diane Dillon, illustrators
Knopf, 1993

When the Thirteenth Amendment to the Constitution was ratified in 1865, four million African Americans were released from slavery. Former slaves fighting for the Union Army in the Civil War sang "No More Auction Block for Me" as they marched, with its chorus "Many thousand gone…" referring to all the people who had suffered the horrors of slavery. In this book, Virginia Hamilton tells this story and thirty-three others—stories of people forced into slavery, people surviving slavery, people helping others escape slavery, President Lincoln declaring all enslaved peoples to be free, and escaped slaves fighting in uniform against their former owners. Covering 1699 to 1866, Virginia Hamilton's stories are based in fact, with just enough speculation to create a moving narrative. Her stories are inspiring, as is the resiliency of a people who survived one of the biggest injustices in our nation's history. Many of the stories have abrupt time and action changes, which are successfully signaled by masterful use of punctuation and paragraphing.

Strange Happenings
Avi
Harcourt, Inc., 2006

In each of the five short stories in this collection, someone gets exactly what he or she asked for, unfortunately. In "Bored Tom," twelve-year-old Tom Pitshugh changes places with a talking cat, for much longer than he intended. In "Babette, the Beautiful," a powerful queen strikes a deal with a witch. "Curious" follows twelve-year-old Jeff Marley as he attempts to find out who is inside the alien costume worn by the mascot of his home team, the Rolerton Astros. In "The Shoemaker and Old Scratch," an attempt to outwit the Devil ends up like most attempts of that nature seem to. In "Simon," a self-centered man wants the whole world to notice of him. When he kills the most beautiful bird on earth, the world does, indeed, take notice, but for all the wrong reasons. Avi's stories read like old fairy tales in modern language, each with a compelling conflict and a rewarding resolution in which the protagonist is punished for his or her sins. Avi is careful to signal speaker changes with correct punctuation and paragraphing.

Love Me, Love My Broccoli

Julie Anne Peters
Avon Books, 1999

Chloe Mankewicz has a lot to do: save the world's endangered bird species, promote recycling, fight for animal rights, and maintain a vegetarian diet. She does spend some of her time, however, on less noble pursuits, like watching through her window Brett Ryan, football and wrestling star, mow her neighbor's yard, while wishing she had some way to get to know him. And then one day, it happens: He approaches her. Brett asks for help on a letter he is writing to the governor about gun control, a topic close to Chloe's heart. She is cool and collected, until Brett asks her on a date. A relationship begins to flower. As Chloe grows closer to Brett, she spends less time campaigning for the Earth and more time attending Brett's football games. But Chloe's conscience is powerful. When controversy over animal testing splits the community, she knows she must do the right thing, Brett or no Brett. Will he understand? As subtle and not-so-subtle changes occur in characters' opinions, Peters maintains clarity with good use of punctuation and paragraphing.

Bury My Heart at Wounded Knee: An Indian History of the American West

Dee Brown
Amy Ehrlich, adaptor
Henry Holt, 1993

The arrival European colonists set into motion America's own holocaust, the genocide of its indigenous people. The majority of Native Americans died of diseases introduced by the colonists, but a great number were killed in military action or starved to death when their hunting grounds were overtaken. This book details the tragedy that befell the Native American nations of the western United States during the second half of the 19th century. Broken treaties, broken trust, and the unscrupulous coveting and stealing of promised lands are black marks on the history of the United States. In this account, adapted for teen readers by Amy Ehrlich, Brown reveals tragic truths about the demise of America's indigenous people, including the abusive treatment waged by the United States Army in the so-called "Indian Wars." Brown relies heavily on punctuation marks as signposts to chronicle accurately the intricacies of the story and the treachery of the Europeans. (Mature Themes)

Key Quality: Capitalizing Correctly

Code Blue: Calling All Capitals!

Pamela Hall
Gary Currant, illustrator
Magic Wagon, 2009

The clinic is in chaos! The receptionist has a cold and calls in sick. Everything is going smoothly until Nurse Germ, the receptionist's temporary replacement, decides she has no need for capital letters. As a result, patients' names, important dates, delivery notices, and lab orders become one big muddled mess. As a last resort to restore order, Nurse Germ calls Dr. Parr, who is enjoying a day off on the golf course. Can he help? Read the book to find out! *Code Blue: Calling All Capitals!* is part of the Grammar's Slammin' series, picture books that bring to life the sometimes stuffy topic of conventions. Each book tells a lighthearted story inspired by a particular convention and, in the back, provides guidelines for writers to remember as they compose. The series is sure to jump-start and maintain your students' commitment to following rules—and breaking them for good reason.

Explorer

Rupert Matthews
Dorling Kindersley, 2005

Explorer is part of DK's Eyewitness Books series, which has become a well-deserving fixture in most school libraries. We chose it as a great book for modeling capitalization because every conceivable capitalization rule is represented: names of people (Magellan, Earhart, Armstrong), names of places (Cape Horn, Arctic Ocean, Oregon Trail), nationalities (Roman, Polynesian, Scandinavian), and many others. By sharing the book with students, you'll give them not only a clear lesson on conventions, but also an introduction to the fascinating world of exploration, from the ancient Phoenicians to the NASA astronauts. They'll learn big facts, such as the reason Columbus set out on his daring voyage, and small ones, such as James Cook's thoughts on kangaroos. They'll travel to all points on the world map, through land, sea, and air. And, of course, they'll enjoy the stunning photography, the trademark of all Eyewitness Books.

Black Star, Bright Dawn

Scott O'Dell
Houghton Mifflin, 1988

Bartok was the *"an-yai-yu-kok,"* the leader of his Inuit village on the Bering Sea, on the west coast of Alaska, but when he is stranded on an ice floe during a seal hunt, he is badly frostbitten and suffers a debilitating phobia of the cold. Out of dread for the frozen sea, Bartok moves his family 40 miles inland to Ikuma, a place very different from his family's home village on the sea.

His daughter, Bright Dawn, finds the new and mixed cultural influences confusing and somewhat disturbing. She learns of "heaven and hellfire" in the town church, and her father takes on a miserable job in a cannery. Bartok turns out to be a champion dogsled racer, however, and the town drafts him to be their representative in the Iditarod, the famed 1200-mile race from Anchorage to Nome. When Bartok is injured while training, Bright Dawn, now eighteen, takes over, and so begins the grandest adventure of her life. Can she and her strong-willed lead dog, Black Star, really compete against veteran mushers from all over Alaska and Canada? Inuit words, such as *Oteg*; dog names, such as Raven; titles, such as Reverend; company names, such as Empire Canning Company; and First Nation names, such as Tlingit, call for careful attention to capitalization.

Dump Trucks and Dogsleds: I'm on My Way, Mom!

Henry Winkler and Lin Oliver
Grosset and Dunlap, 2009

Hank Zipzer is not pleased about the prospect of sharing his room with a new baby brother. So his dad tries to appease him by taking him and his sister, Emily, on ski trip to Vermont, while their mom stays in New York City in case the baby arrives early. And, sure enough, he does! When she goes into labor and is rushed to the hospital, Hank, Emily, and Dad attempt to drive back to NYC, only to be sidelined by a major snowstorm. A train ride in a freight car full of horses gets them partway home, and a van filled with Chinese acrobats gets them further. After that, they hitch a ride on a dog sled into the Bronx, followed by a cab to the hospital. Hank and his parents have a healthy relationship, and the authors' portrayal of resolving problems within a family is encouraging. New England place names call for careful use of capital letters.

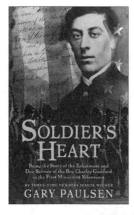

Soldier's Heart: A Novel of the Civil War

Gary Paulsen
Delacorte, 1998

Based on the life of Charley Goddard, a fifteen-year-old Minnesotan who fought in the Battle of Bull Run, this story brings the horrors of the Civil War to life. Paulsen shows, in poignant, sometimes graphic detail how the boy and his comrades were placed in harm's way again and again, with deadly consequence for most of them. He presents facts, as recorded in text and pictures, about soldiers left to die on the battlefields because medicine was so primitive at the time. Readers will understand perfectly why Charley survived those battlefields but died at home in Minnesota not long after his return, of a damaged nervous and circulatory system from what was then called "soldier's heart," or Da Costa's Syndrome, a condition caused by constantly fighting for life under the hopeless conditions of war. Names of people, places, and battles up the ante on correct use of capitalization, which Paulsen achieves. (Mature Themes)

Conventions

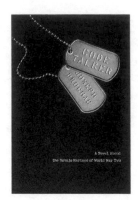

Code Talkers: A Novel About the Navajo Marines of World War Two
Joseph Bruchac
Speak, 2006

Native American author Joseph Bruchac tells the story of Ned Begay, a Navajo code talker in World War II. At age six, Ned was sent away to boarding school, where Native American children were forbidden to speak in their native language under threat of punishment. Ironically, ten years later, Ned would find himself in the United States Marine Corps, using his native language, or the "unbreakable code," to help the United States defeat the Japanese and bring peace to the world. The code allowed the American forces to communicate openly on radio channels, calling in fire from ships at sea and coordinating assaults on enemy positions without fear of enemy decoding. The narrator describes some of the desperate battles fought to gain control of the Pacific Theater, including Guadalcanal, Bougainville, and Iwo Jima, always weaving in Navajo philosophy and perspectives. Accurate capitalization of unfamiliar proper nouns in English, Japanese, and Navajo helps readers move through the book.

Key Quality: Applying Grammar and Usage

The Word Fun Series
Michael Dahl and Nancy Loewen
Sara Gray, illustrator
Picture Window Books, 2006 and 2007

In our estimation, any well-written picture book can be used to model grammar and usage. But if you want to teach students specific concepts, look no further than the Word Fun series:

If You Were an Adjective, Dahl

If You Were an Adverb, Dahl

If You Were an Antonym, Loewen

If You Were a Conjunction, Loewen

If You Were a Noun, Dahl

If You Were a Preposition, Loewen

If You Were a Synonym, Dahl

If You Were a Verb, Dahl

Each one packs a pedagogical punch. Your students will likely get the concept immediately, begin applying it to their own work, and have a laugh in the process.

Matilda

Roald Dahl
Penguin, 1988

Matilda Wormwood is precocious. She teaches herself to read by age three and, by four, she has devoured every children's book in the public library and has started on the classics. Not all the adults in Matilda's life, unfortunately, are equally enlightened. Her father, a dishonest used-car salesman, thinks she should be watching more television. Her mother thinks bingo and TV dinners are mainstays of civilization. Matilda's school is run by Miss Trunchbull, "a gigantic, holy terror" who marches through the halls, plowing through anyone who stands in her way. But then there is Miss Honey, Matilda's teacher, who loves her students dearly. When Matilda discovers that Miss Trunchbull raised Miss Honey from the age of five, she hatches a plot that ensures Miss Honey, rather than Miss Trunchbull, receives the family fortune. Stickler for correctness that she is, Matilda would never accept bad grammar!

Slam!

Walter Dean Myers
Scholastic, 1996

Greg Harris's father is out of work and drinking excessively, his grandmother is dying, and Greg (a.k.a. "Slam") himself is flunking out of school. The only place where the seventeen-year-old has any modicum of control over his world is on a basketball court. Even though he has just transferred to a magnet school where students have a much higher probability than those in his previous school of succeeding in life beyond high school, he seems to be on a path of self-destruction. Before the book ends, Slam will figure out what things are beyond his control, what things are within his control, and how to be the best person he can be. Walter Dean Myers proves again that he is a master of portraying the complex lives of young African-American men, without resorting to stereotypes or heavy-handed messages. Differences between dialectal and standard English are underscored by grammar and usage.

I Am a Star: Child of the Holocaust
Inge Auerbacher
Penguin, 1993

Out of 15,000 children who entered the Terezin Concentration Camp, Auerbacher was one of only 100 children who survived. Weaving together her poetry, photographs of her life, and drawings by illustrator Israel Bernbaum, Auerbacher tells the story of her life, beginning in Germany before World War II and continuing through her family's imprisonment and their immigration to the United States after the war. Auerbacher's frightful transition from a happy, stable, middle-class existence in the small city of Kippenheim, Germany, to a horrifying existence in Terezin, where death awaited the majority of prisoners, is explained straightforwardly and unflinchingly. The spirit of the young narrator burns brightly, from start to finish. This is a great nonfiction work to couple with a fictional Holocaust account, such as *Number the Stars*. A nonnative speaker of English, Auerbacher was especially careful to make the book's grammar and usage perfect.

Men on the Moon
Simon J. Ortiz
University of Arizona Press, 1999

Simon Ortiz presents a collection of 26 short stories that focus on the life and times of indigenous people in the Southwest. In the title story, Faustin, an elderly grandfather, receives a TV from his daughter just in time to see the Apollo 13 rocket launch. Faustin watches the NASA liftoff and asks a logical question, "Are those men looking for something on the moon?" The astronauts, he learns, are looking for knowledge on the moon, which makes him wonder if they had "run out of places to look for knowledge on the earth." He is perplexed by the fact that the astronauts are interested in finding out if there is even "the tiniest bit of life" on the moon, but that they are also afraid that what they find might be dangerous and so the men are quarantined upon returning. Ortiz's stories are carefully and concisely crafted. Every word carries important meaning, meaning that reveals much about the Native American experience in particular and the human experience in general. Ortiz keeps his themes at the center, maintaining simple, correct grammar and usage throughout. (Mature Themes)

Author Index

Abdel-Fattah, Randa, 99,107–109

Alexie, Sherman, 52, 58, 66–68

Anderson, Laurie Halse, 19

Aston, Diane Hutts, 82

Auerbacher, Inge, 126

Avi, 60, 120

Barakat, Ibtisam, 98

Bartone, Elisa, 14

Bauer, Joan, 24

Baylor, Byrd, 97

Beatty, Patricia, 21

Bloor, Edward, 23

Blundell, Judy, 63

Bradbury, Ray, 88

Brooks, Bruce, 9

Brown, Dee,121

Bruchac, Joseph, 61, 124

Bunting, Eve, 14

Carman, Patrick, 35

Carr, Jan, 116, 119–120

Carson, Rachel, 41

Cisneros, Sandra,23–24, 30–31

Colfer, Eoin,42–43

Collins, Suzanne, 7, 78–79,87–88

Connor, Leslie, 81

Cooney, Caroline B., 101

Courlander, Harold, 58

Coville, Bruce, 62–63

Creech, Sharon, 117

Dahl, Michael, 124

Dahl, Roald, 42, 125

DiCamillo, Kate,80

Draper, Sharon M., 38, 60

DuPrau, Jeanne, 118

Earley, Tony, 72, 76, 85–86

Ehrlich, Amy, 41, 121

Elliott, David, 63

Flake, Sharon G., 43, 49–50

Fogelin, Adrian, 40

Funke, Cornelia, 95

Gaiman, Neil, 15, 56

Gantos, Jack, 24

Graham, Ian, 59

Green, Tim, 100, 109–111

Gutman, Dan, 57–58

Haarsma, PJ, 35–36, 44–45

Hall, Donald, 54, 64–65

Hall, Pamela, 122

Hamilton, Virginia, 120

Hatkoff, Craig, 20

Hatkoff, Isabella, 20

Hatkoff, Juliana, 20

Herrera, Juan Felipe, 78

Herzog, George, 58

Hesse, Karen, 77, 84, 92, 103, 112–113

Hiassen, Carl, 64

Hobbs, Will, 41, 118

Horvath, Polly, 78, 103

Hunter, Sara Hoagland, 12, 22

Jackson, Shirley, 88

Johnson, Maureen, 18

Kadohata, Cynthia, 21, 28–29

Kerley, Barbara, 80

Konigsberg, Bill, 96

Korman, Gordon, 15, 25–26

Laden, Nina, 74

Landy, Derek, 75

Langan, Paul, 59

Lee, Harper, 72, 76

Le Guin, Ursula K., 79

Lethcoe, Jason, 83–84

Levine, Ellen, 17

Lipsyte, Robert, 98

Loewen, Nancy, 124

Loh, Virginia Shin-Mui, 95

Lord, Cynthia, 61, 68–70

Lowry, Lois, 55, 88

Macaulay, David, 72, 82, 90–91

Marsalis, Wynton, 100

Marsden, Carolyn, 95

Matthews, Rupert, 122

McCully, Emily Arnold, 36

McLimans, David, 34

McPhail, David, 42

Mendez, Phil, 60

Miller, Heather Lynn, 62, 70–71

Monninger, Joseph, 96

Moss, Marissa, 34

Myers, Walter Dean, 16, 125

Naylor, Phyllis Reynolds, 98

Noble, Trinka Hakes, 19, 39, 47–49

Nye, Naomi Shihab, 99

O'Dell, Scott, 122–123

Oliver, Lin, 123

O'Malley, Kevin, 102

Ortiz, Simon, 126

Park, Linda Sue, 100

Paulsen, Gary, 43, 104, 123

Peck, Richard, 37, 46–47

Peters, Julie Anne, 121

Philbrick, Rodman, 81

Polacco, Patricia, 52, 57

Prior, Natalie Jane, 32, 42

Pullman, Phillip, 12, 18

Qamar, Amjed, 53, 56

Rallison, Janette, 101

Raskin, Ellen, 37–38

Ritter, John, 103–104

Ryan, Pam Muñoz, 80–81, 88–90

Rylant, Cynthia, 23, 37

Sachar, Louis, 32, 34–35

Shetterly, Robert, 79

Shulman, Mark, 116

Sís, Peter, 39

Skármeta, Antonio, 17, 26–28

Sleator, William, 75

Smith Jr., Charles R., 74

Smith, Cynthia Leitich, 16

Smith, Lane, 62

Soto, Gary, 40, 83

Stead, Rebecca, 55

Sterling, Shirley, 118–119

Stiefvater, Maggie, 22

Terban, Marvin, 116, 117

Testa, Maria, 20

Truss, Lynne, 116, 119

Turner, Megan Whalen, 36

Uhlich, Gerald R., 20

Villareal, Ray, 38

Waboose, Jan Bourdeau, 97

Westerfeld, Scott, 83

Whitman, Walt, 77

Winkler, Henry, 123

Winter, Jonah, 57

Wood, Douglas, 94

Woodruff, Elvira, 54

Woodson, Jacqueline, 102

Yang, Gene, 32, 40–41, 95

Yee, Lisa, 17–18

Yolen, Jane, 94, 105–107

Young, Ed, 9–10

Title Index

Absolutely True Diary of a Part-Time Indian, The, Alexie, 52, 58, 66–68

American Born Chinese, Yang, 32, 40–41, 95

Americans Who Tell the Truth, Shetterly, 79

Angel for Solomon Singer, An, Rylant, 23

Beautiful Warrior, McCully, 36

Because of Winn-Dixie, DiCamillo, 80

Becoming Joe DiMaggio, Testa, 20

Becoming Naomi León, Ryan, 80–81, 88–90

Beneath My Mother's Feet, Qamar, 53, 56

Black Snowman, The, Mendez, 60

Black Star, Bright Dawn, O'Dell, 122–123

Bloomability, Creech, 117

Blue Star, The, Earley, 72, 76, 85–86

Bully, The, Langan, 59

Bury My Heart at Wounded Knee: An Indian History of the American West, Brown, 121

Catcher in the Rye, The, Salinger, 109

Catching Fire, Collins, 7

Chains, Anderson, 19

Charlotte's Web, White, 45

Cinnamon Girl, Herrera, 78

City of Ember, The, DuPrau, 118

Code Blue: Calling All Capitals! Hall, 120

Code Talkers, Bruchac, 124

Composition, The, Skármeta, 17, 26–28

Coraline, Gaiman, 56

Cow-Tail Switch and Other West African Stories, The, Courlander & Herzog, 58

Cracker! The Best Dog in Vietnam, Kadohata, 21, 28–29

Crossing Jordan, Fogelin, 40

Dark Hills Divide, The, Carman, 35

Day No Pigs Would Die, A, Newton, 109

Dinosaurs of Waterhouse Hawkins, The, Kerley, 80

Does My Head Look Big in This? Abdel-Fattah, 99, 107–109

Dove Dove: Funny Homograph Riddles, The, Terban, 117

Down the Yukon, Hobbs, 118

Downriver, Hobbs, 41

Dump Trucks and Dogsleds: I'm on My Way, Mom! Winkler & Oliver, 123

Eats, Shoots & Leaves, Truss, 119

Eight Ate: A Feast of Homonym Riddles, Terban, 116, 117

Egg Is Quiet, An, Aston, 82

Everything on a Waffle, Horvath

Explorer, Matthews, 122

Fabulous Feud of Gilbert & Sullivan, The, Winter, 57

Face on the Milk Carton, The, Cooney, 101

Fahrenheit 451, Bradbury, 109

Football Genius, Green, 100, 109–111

Forged by Fire, Draper, 38

Gathering Blue, Lowry, 55

Girl's Like Spaghetti, The, Truss, 119

Giver, The, Lowry, 55, 88, 109

Golden Compass, The, Pullman, 12, 18

Gone Wild: An Endangered Alphabet, McLimans, 34

Graveyard Book, The, Gaiman, 15

Greatest: Muhammad Ali, The, Myers, 16

Greedy Apostrophe: A Cautionary Tale, Carr, 116, 119 120

Green Futures of Tycho, The, Sleator, 75

Hannah's Journal, Moss, 34

Harry Potter and the Sorcerer's Stone, Rowling, 45

Henry's Freedom Box, Levine, 17

Hippie Chick, Monninger, 96

Holes, Sachar, 32, 34–35

Hoot, Hiassen, 64

House on Mango Street, The, Cisneros, 23–24, 30–31

Hunger Games, The, Collins, 78–79, 87–88

I Am a Star: Child of the Holocaust, Auerbacher, 126

I Am the Dog, I Am the Cat, Hall, 54, 64–65

I Know Why the Caged Bird Sings, Angelou, 109

I Was a Sixth Grade Alien, Coville, 62–65

If You Were a Conjunction, Loewen, 124

If You Were a Noun, Dahl, 124

If You Were a Preposition, Loewen, 124

If You Were a Synonym, Dahl, 124

If You Were a Verb, Dahl, 124

If You Were an Adjective, Dahl, 124

If You Were an Adverb, Dahl, 124

If You Were an Antonym, Loewen, 124

In a Pickle: And Other Funny Idioms, Terban, 117

Inkheart, Funke, 95

Instead of Three Wishes, Turner, 36

Jack's Black Book, Gantos, 24

Jade Dragon, The, Marsden & Loh, 95

Jason's Gold, Hobbs, 118

Jazz ABZ: An A to Z Collection of Jazz Portraits, Marsalis, 100

Jim the Boy, Earley, 76, 85

Jim Thorpe, Original All-American, Bruchac, 61

John, Paul, George & Ben, Smith, 62

Journey: Stories of Migration, The, Rylant, 37

Jurassic Park, Crichten, 80

Knut: How One Little Polar Bear Captivated the World, J. Hatkoff, I. Hatkoff, C. Hatkoff & Uhlich, 20

Last Book in the Universe, The, Philbrick, 81

Legend of Spud Murphy, The, Colfer, 42–43

Letters From Rifka, Hesse, 84

Life, Love, and the Pursuit of Free Throws, Rallison, 101

Lily Quench and the Black Mountains, Prior, 32, 42

Long Way from Chicago, A, Peck, 37

Love Me, Love My Broccoli, Peters, 121

Lupita Mañana, Beatty, 21

Many Thousand Gone: African Americans From Slavery to Freedom, Hamilton, 120

Matilda, Dahl, 42, 125

Meanwhile Back at the Ranch, Noble, 39, 47–49

Memory Coat, The, Woodruff, 54

Men on the Moon, Ortiz, 126

Million Dollar Kick, The, Gutman, 57–58

Misadventures of Benjamin Bartholomew Piff: Wishful Thinking, The, Lethcoe, 83

Missing May, Rylant, 23

Mom and Dad Are Palindromes, Shulman, 116

Morning on the Lake, Waboose, 97

Motel of the Mysteries, Macaulay, 72, 82, 90–91

Moves Make the Man, The, Brooks, 9

Music of Dolphins, The, Hesse, 92, 103, 112–113

My Father, the Angel of Death, Villareal, 38

My Life in Dog Years, Paulsen, 43

My Name Is Seepeetza, Sterling, 118–119

Nightjohn, Paulsen, 104

No! McPhail, 42

No More Dead Dogs, Korman, 15, 25–26

Number the Stars, Lowry, 126

Old Turtle, Wood, 94

Old Turtle and the Broken Truth, Wood, 94

Old Yeller, Fred Gipson, 15, 26

Once Upon a Cool Motorcycle Dude, O'Malley, 102

Orange Shoes, The, Noble, 19

Out of the Pocket, Konigsberg, 96

Owen & Mzee: The True Story of a Remarkable Friendship, I. Hatkoff, C. Hatkoff, Kahumbu & Greste, 20

Owl Moon, Yolen, 94, 105–107

Pacific Crossing, Soto, 40

Peppe the Lamplighter, Bartone, 14

Perloo the Bold, Avi, 60

Pink and Say, Polacco, 52, 57

Pop's Bridge, Bunting, 14

Rachel: The Story of Rachel Carson, Ehrlich, 41

Rain Is Not My Indian Name, Smith, 16

Romeow and Drooliet, Laden, 74

Rules, Lord, 61, 68–70

Sassy: Little Sister Is Not My Name, Draper, 60

Seed Is Sleepy, A, Aston, 82

Seven Blind Mice, Young, 9–10

Shiloh, Naylor, 98

Shiver, Stiefvater, 22

Show Way, Woodson, 102

Silent Spring, 41

Single Shard, A, Park, 100

Sitti's Secrets, Nye, 99

Skin I'm In, The, Flake, 43, 49–50

Skirt, The, Soto, 83

Skulduggery Pleasant, Landy, 75

Slam! Myers, 125

Softwire: Virus on Orbis I, The, Haarsma, 35–36, 44–45

Soldier's Heart, Paulsen, 123

Sounder, Armstrong, 15, 26

Spuds, Hesse, 77

Squashed, Bauer, 24

Stanford Wong Flunks Big Time, Yee, 17–18

Strange Happenings, Avi, 120

Suite Scarlett, Johnson, 18

Table Where Rich People Sit, The, Baylor, 97

Tangerine, Bloor, 23

Tasting the Sky, Barakat, 98

Tears of a Tiger, Draper, 38

This Is Your Life Cycle, Miller, 62, 70–71

To Kill a Mockingbird, Lee, 72, 76

Transmogrification of Roscoe Wizzle, The, Elliott, 63

Twelve Rounds to Glory: The Story of Muhammad Ali, Smith Jr., 74

Twenty-Odd Ducks: Why, Every Punctuation Mark Counts! Truss, 116, 119

Uglies, Westerfeld, 83–84

Unbreakable Code, The, Hunter, 12, 22

Under the Baseball Moon, Ritter, 103–104

Waiting for Normal, Connor, 81

Wall: Growing Up Behind the Iron Curtain, The, Sís, 39

Warrior Angel, Lipsyte, 98

Westing Game, The, Raskin, 37–38

What I Saw and How I Lied, Blundell, 63

When I Heard the Learn'd Astronomer, Whitman, 77

When the Circus Came to Town, Horvath, 103

When You Reach Me, Stead, 55

Where the Red Fern Grows, W. Rawls & W. Rawls, 26, 45

Wizard of Earthsea, A, Le Guin, 79

Wrinkle in Time, A, L'Engle, 55

Year Down Yonder, A, Peck, 37, 46–47

You Wouldn't Want to Be on Apollo 13! A Mission You'd Rather Not Go On, Graham, 59

References

Brooks, B. (1990). Bruce Brooks. In D. Gallo (Ed.). *Speaking for ourselves: Autobiographical sketches by notable authors of books for young adults.* Urbana, IL: National Council Teachers of English.

Dorfman, L. R., & Cappelli, R. (2007). *Mentor texts: Teaching writing through children's literature, K–6.* Portland, Maine: Stenhouse.

Escribano, P. D. (1999). Teaching writing through reading: a text-centered approach. Retrieved October 23, 2009, from http://www.aelfe.org//documents/text1-Duran.pdf

Hall, D., & Emblen, D. L. (1994). *A writer's reader* (seventh edition). New York: HarperCollins College Publishers.

King, S. (2000). *On writing: A memoir of the craft.* New York: Scribner.

Lamott, A. (1994). *Bird by bird: Some instructions on writing and life.* New York: Random House.

Murray, D. (1985). *A writer teaches writing.* Boston: Houghton Mifflin Company.

Off the Mark. October 3, 2003. Spelling cartoon 13 of 28. Retrieved November 7, 2009 from http://www.offthemark.com/searchresults.php?topic=none&keywords=spelling&resultsfrom=11&browseall=false

Ray, K. W. (1999). *Wondrous words: Writers and writing in the elementary classroom.* Urbana, Illinois: National Council Teachers of English.

Scott, C. (2008). How to create a strong ending in fiction. eHow. Retrieved May 19, 2010, from http://www.ehow.com/how_4556278_create-strong-ending-fiction.html

Zinsser, W. (2001). *On writing well* (sixth edition). New York: HarperCollins.